BABEL

versus

BIBLE

The Battle for the Heart of Mankind

DAVID J LAMBOURN

DEDICATION

To all seekers after God's Kingdom and Glory

CONTENTS

ACKNOWLEDGEMENTS

I would like to acknowledge with profound thanks the constant support of my family, friends and Hope Community Church, along with many other dear Christian friends in the writing of this book. In particular, I owe a special debt of gratitude to Peter Sammons of Christian Publications International, along with Simon Pease and Peter Donoghue, for their careful checking through of material and invaluable suggestions for improving the text, and to Alex Jacob for supplying such a generous preface.

Most of all, I would like to thank our great and incomparable God for his wonderful revelation, guidance and direction over the whole project. In him the tangled threads of history weave together into a tapestry that we will never fully comprehend, but which reveals breathtaking beauty and power, in the midst of both tragedy and triumph. To him be glory for ever and ever!

PREFACE

How should Christians engage constructively with the world and in so doing reflect and model the example of Jesus?

This is a huge and highly significant question; a question that inevitably throws up a vast array of possible 'answers'. In trying to navigate a helpful path through this array of possible answers, a worthwhile starting point will be this new book by David Lambourn.

The author gives a perceptive and penetrating overview of Biblical history and provides valuable resources for helping develop a 'Christian worldview'. This 'worldview' engages faithfully with - and robustly challenges - many strands of contemporary culture. David Lambourn writes with clarity and detailed insight, yet his book remains very accessible.

The sweep of Biblical texts and stories are impressive. The 'Questions to Consider' concluding each chapter are well chosen and bring about much helpful group discussion as well as personal reflection and a stimulus for further study and action. I warmly commend the book on this basis.

Rev. Alex Jacob

CEO The Church's Ministry among Jewish People (CMJ)

INTRODUCTION

As I finish this book, the world is still struggling to emerge from one of its greatest challenges for a generation. For the best part of two years humanity has seemingly been held to ransom by a completely invisible foe that at times has threatened to bring vital segments of civilisation to a standstill. This unfolding saga has produced an extraordinary range of responses: some have had their lives knocked sideways; many have been paralysed by fear, while others have gone about their normal lives as if nothing had happened.

Every crisis tells a bigger story. What we have seen in the natural is but a tiny picture of the spiritual assault that rages against humanity every day. Unseen supernatural forces bombard us incessantly and yet, while many are knocked out or paralysed by their attacks, multitudes live in total denial that such forces exist at all. As with the indiscriminate onslaught of a virus, their power lies in remaining completely hidden from human eyes, and yet having the capacity (if left unchecked) to infect vast numbers of people on the planet. And so often the symptoms lie dormant and are virtually undetectable, until it is too late to stop their invisible but explosive spread.

The Bible is the only book in existence which gives us a real insight into this battle. Throughout the pages of scripture we see two spiritual kingdoms wrestling head-to-head against each other. The struggle between these kingdoms has dominated history and continues to impact the world around us to this very day. Moreover, it often spills over into our own lives, with subtle forces attempting to seize control of our individual thoughts, actions and decisions. We need to gain insight into this conflict if we are to achieve victory in the many challenges that we face in our Christian walk.

Today, many believers are ill-equipped to face this battle. So often we are caught unawares, spiritually loitering and with a dwindling supply of oil in our lamps. All too frequently we fail to discern the tactics and schemes of the enemy.

Many others, however, are all too aware of this struggle and feel overwhelmed. It is all too easy to become frustrated and discouraged in the face of an apparently unstoppable tide. Some, like Elijah at Mount Horeb, feel like giving up completely and deserting the battlefield for good (1 Kings 19.10).

Yet in all these situations there is hope. Many have drawn inspiration from the story of David and Goliath in the Old Testament. With only meagre resources at his disposal against seemingly impossible odds, an unknown and apparently ill-prepared youth vanquishes a colossal bully. This perennial favourite among Bible passages has inspired many believers as they battle giants in their own lives, with nothing to fall back on but the tiniest mustard seed of faith, rooted in a God who can achieve anything.

The David and Goliath saga is one that reverberates through much of Israel's history. Over and over again, with all the odds stacked against her, Israel seems to win battles with only tiny resources to draw upon. It happened for Gideon at Moreh (Judges 7.7-25). It happened for Jonathan at Michmash (1 Sam 14.1-23). It happened for Ahab at Samaria against an alliance of 33 kings (1 Kings 20.1-21). It happened for Judas Maccabeus in 166 BC against the entire might of the Seleucid Army. So often in God's economy, less is more.

It has also been evident in the more recent history of the Jewish nation. After the modern state of Israel declared independence in 1948, five Arab nations turned against her in force, but she defeated them single-handedly. In the Yom Kippur War of 1973, she foiled a surprise attack by armies that were numerically vastly superior, and her counter-attack brought her within 60 miles of Cairo and 20 miles of Damascus. And in the first Gulf War of 1991, she survived a barrage of Scud missiles from Iraq where thousands of buildings were hit, and endured only two direct casualties.

On many other occasions, however, the battles have been far less easy. Often Israel has had to fight a prolonged war of attrition against the Goliaths ranged against her. This, for example, was the case in the book of Exodus, against a Pharaoh who stubbornly refused to give ground, despite the unremitting sequence of calamities raining down upon him. And the toughest challenges of all have been against the Goliaths of sin and rebellion that have risen up in Israel's own midst.

These Goliaths are constantly rearing their heads in our own lives as well, but they are symptomatic of a much wider malaise which has impacted our nation, weakened the church, and threatens to alter the direction of Christianity and set it on a new and completely uncharted course.

As we shall see, this rebellion against God is summed up in the word 'Babel' (or its Greek equivalent 'Babylon'), which stands against everything God has planned and purposed for this world, and it goes back to the very dawn of history. Sadly, many of us, blissfully unaware of this seductive and apparently irresistible pull on our lives, find ourselves rushing headlong into its toxic embrace, only to end up trapped in its vice-like grip.

It is for this reason that I have written this book. We will take a look at many of the key events in the Bible, some critical moments in history, and some of the formative trends in the world around us today. We will also consider the spiritual powers in the background that might be pulling strings behind the scenes, and the dire consequences which threaten our institutional churches. In addition, we will attempt to shine God's searchlight on the strongholds in our own hearts.

In attempting to throw light on this conflict, the primary source material that I have used is scripture itself. If we are to allow the Bible to speak into our lives, and to gain victory in the battleground of our minds, we need to receive it as God's direct word to us, without pulling it apart, setting it aside or explaining it away. In the end, absolute change can only come through absolute truth vested in an absolute God. That living word is God's plumbline, against which everything else needs to be measured.

For reference purposes I have, in addition, drawn on a number of other ancient writings, most notably the works of the Jewish historian Flavius Josephus. Where necessary, I have also referred to the work of various more recent authors, as well as other relevant historical sources. All scripture quotations, unless otherwise indicated, are taken from the New International Version of the Bible (2011).[1]

The structure of this book traces out a few twists and turns. The first few chapters are short and largely reflective in style, drawing out how the conflict between kingdoms is birthed in the Old Testament, particularly in the book of Genesis. Towards the middle chapters the atmosphere changes somewhat, as we begin to process significant quantities of historical information. In the last three chapters the threads weave back together again as we spell out the choices we face both within the church and for each of us as individuals, in response to the challenges outlined.

In recent times, as we have seen, the world has been experiencing a period of profound shaking. In the Bible, God allows such times of shaking for a variety of reasons: when mankind has overstepped the mark (Gen. 6.1-7; 19.1-29), after human rebellion has reached a tipping point (Gen. 15.16; Is. 30.13), or when God just wants to remind us who is actually in charge (Gen. 11.6-9; Ps. 2.9). Sometimes he hides his face momentarily, either because we have turned against him (Deut. 31.17) or ignored him (2 Chron. 24.20) or just as a test of our faithfulness (2 Chron. 32.31). And the most significant of the periods of shaking arises in preparation for the coming and return of the Messiah (Haggai 2.6-7).

These seasons of testing are not to imply that God has abandoned us (the opposite is the case), but are simply a powerful reminder that, for all our human bluster and bravado in thinking that we are fully in control of our world, we still wholly depend on his mercy and grace, and we need him back at the centre of our lives. In the West, we have been steadily pushing God out from the heart of our society for almost a century now, heedless of Jesus' stark warning about creating spiritual vacuums which dark powers can all too easily enter and take over (Matt. 12:43-5).

In all these things, we need to be like the men of Issachar, seeking to understand the times in which we live (1 Chron.

12.32). We need to wait upon God to seek his will for our own destiny as individuals, for the church, and for the nations in which we live. Above all, we need his guidance as we grapple with the same choice today that has faced humanity for many centuries. Will we follow the way of Babel? Or will we follow the Bible? This book sets out the consequences of those choices and the battle for the hearts of mankind that has ensued.

Questions to Consider:

(i)   What are the personal Goliaths in our lives and how can we overcome them?

(ii) Read Matthew 17.20, Luke 21.1-4 and John 12.24-25. How do these verses demonstrate the principle that 'less is more'? How can we apply this principle in our day-to-day living?

(iii) What do you think God's purposes are for your community and nation at this time? Where would we most like to see transformation? What would this change look like if we applied it individually in our own lives?

1 A TALE OF TWO CITIES

We all like happy endings. They seem to be hard-wired into our brain. And nothing could be more glorious than the final pages of scripture. The New Jerusalem descends from heaven like a bride adorned for her husband. The gulf between heaven and earth is taken away and God lives for ever with his people.

But happy endings are often birthed in conflict, and the Bible is no exception. The heavenly Jerusalem has an earthly antithesis - her ancient adversary, Babylon. Babylon is the mirror image of the New Jerusalem that turns everything on its head. Instead of descending from heaven, Babylon rises up from the earth. Instead of bringing the goodness of God down into the world, Babylon's sins are piled up as high as the heavens.

There are two clearly contrasting principles at work here. The first reveals how salvation is God's initiative alone: it is something that *he* does for *us*. The second shows mankind's alternative attempt at self-advancement: it is a utopia that *we* attempt to create *on our own*.

The contrast between God's salvation and the corrupt man-centred alternative runs as a theme throughout the entire span of scripture. Back in Genesis 12.2 God tells Abraham, '*I* will make your name great.' But in the previous chapter the builders of Babel (the original name for Babylon) declare, 'let us make a name *for ourselves*' (Gen. 11.4 ESV).

Babylon is always attempting to be *like* God, taking his place, standing in his shoes, calling the shots. It is an attempt to establish a do-it-yourself scheme of 'salvation' and an artificial paradise by earthly means, keeping God himself out of the equation.

Ultimately the original architect of such a vision is not hard to find. Behind the bold statements from 'the king of Babylon' chapter 14 of Isaiah it is not difficult to hear the shrill tones of Satan himself:

> '*I* will ascend to the heavens;
> I will raise my throne
>   above the stars of God;
> I will sit enthroned on the mount of assembly,
>   on the utmost heights of Mount Zaphon.
> I will ascend above the tops of the clouds;
> I will make myself like the Most High.' (Is. 14.13-14)

Likewise, the prophecy about the king of Tyre in Ezekiel 28 seems to resonate with echoes of Satan's own fall from grace:

> 'Son of man, say to the ruler of Tyre, "This is what the Sovereign LORD says:
>
> ' "In the pride of your heart
>   you say, '*I* am a god;
> I sit on the throne of a god
>   in the heart of the seas." ' (Ezek. 28.2)

And yet, set against these, we have a startlingly different example that calls out to us:

> Christ Jesus … being in very nature God,
>   did not consider equality with God something to be used to
> his own advantage;
> rather, **he made himself nothing**
>   by taking the very nature of a servant,
>   being made in human likeness.
> And being found in appearance as a man,
>   he humbled himself
>   by becoming obedient to death –
>   even death on a cross! (Phil. 2.5-8)

The incarnation of Christ, then, is the exact opposite of Isaiah chapter 14. Both trace two diametrically opposed trajectories: the first is the one Satan invites us to follow in the Garden of Eden; the second is the one Jesus invites us to follow in the Garden of Gethsemane.

While Satan constantly magnifies himself, Christ's life is marked by servanthood. Outside the unique 'I am' statements, Jesus often deflects attention away from himself, and frequently strives to conceal the truth of his Messiahship, not to mention his divine origins. Despite being King of Kings, he lived his life in humility and simplicity and died in agony and humiliation on a wooden cross.

The life of Jesus presents us with a truly authentic template for human existence in all its highs and lows. It demonstrates life in all its fulness, as it was really intended to be lived.

And yet today, as we look around at every aspect of our culture, we see the fingerprints of the opposite worldview. It is a counter-kingdom diametrically opposed to the principles that Jesus taught, and its roots stretch right back to the very dawn of history itself.

One of the main distinctive attitudes of Babylon is **self-exaltation**. In this worldview man is at the centre of everything. He is enthroned as his own god and can fulfil his own destiny through sheer determination and willpower. Constantly seeking to advance himself and make a name for himself, he erects great structures that rise up like artificial mountains - pyramids, ziggurats, or, in our own day, soaring tower blocks, to write that upward quest permanently into the landscape that surrounds him. Through display and showmanship he tries to project success, glory and bravura, always centring on the need to 'look good'. All, however, is cosmetic and ultimately hollow, the triumph of outward appearance over inner substance.

Wedded to this outward show is a relentless battle for power, wealth and status. Left unchecked, it is only the toughest who survive: the weakest go to the wall. It is a race to win in which the young and the strong gain the upper hand at the expense of the elderly, the weak and the marginalised. Tradition and deference, the marks of gentler and more traditional rural societies, are seen as signs of weakness. The pursuit of power becomes a game of chess where each move displays a calculated ruthlessness, brutality concealed in a velvet glove.

As a counterpoint to this rugged individualism lies an unshaken belief in **self-sufficiency**. Man can survive without God and instead possesses the keys of his own salvation. This tempers the drive towards individualism with the need to act together in solidarity. In his heart man longs for the New Jerusalem, for which he has been created and towards which everything within him unconsciously aspires. He instinctively strives to emulate this by creating something inspiring and beautiful which can supply every need. But without God he must achieve this by himself.

No doubt this drive brings out many of the nobler qualities of mankind. It has produced great works of art and music and extraordinary strides forward in science and technology. It has stirred up many noble acts of altruism and many imaginative social welfare schemes. But artificial attempts to create utopia, as we see, for example, in Communism, are doomed in the end to fail because they are spiritually bankrupt. They have no lasting value because existence has no ultimate purpose. 'Meaningless! Meaningless!' is the damning verdict of Ecclesiastes.

Behind this lies a wider principle of **self-containment**. The city - the nucleus for nation states, empires, or the global village we know today - was in its original conception a closed unit, operating on its own internal networks of communication, contained within protective walls. It had its own systems of taxation, administration and commerce and its own sphere of influence. By inculcating into everyone a basic hunger for a better future, higher social standing and a better standard of living, it relentlessly drove itself forward like a well-oiled machine. Through the soft arm of trade or the hard fist of military conquest, it became possible to steadily extend influence and annex more and more power and wealth from elsewhere.

Today, this principle of self-containment extends to every level of society. Human beings have become cogs in this machine, valued only for what they can produce and what they can spend. All commodities - money, goods, sex, music - become ends in themselves, existing for their own sake. And within this scheme we ourselves have become machines in our own right. With God dethroned from his rightful position, body, mind, personality, and anything that makes us distinctively human is devalued. We become nothing more than a bundle of chemicals with no intrinsic value or ultimate meaning.

The same is true of the way we see the world itself. Through some abstract process of 'nature' (the word has no existence in Hebrew, as everything was seen as being the direct action of God), mankind happily seems to accept that all things *brought themselves* into being. The investigation of knowledge stops at 'how?' as the question 'why?' has been ruled out of court. Even the universe itself has been reduced to another self-designing machine, an idea explicitly ruled out by scripture (Is. 10.15; 29.16; Jer. 14.22). The cosmos, in a sense, has become its own Babylon!

Given the spiritual void that this produces, man is inevitably driven into an endless quest for **self-fulfilment**. The tragedy of Babylon is that self-exaltation and other forms of self-centredness mask a fundamental insecurity. The defiant claim that '*I am*, and there is none besides me' (Isaiah 47.8) conceals the real inner question, 'Who *am* I'? In Eden, as we shall see, identity is defined by relationship with God and with each other. In Babylon, we are defined by our function - *what we do*. Lacking intrinsic value or identity, we are forced to embark on a quest for self-discovery.

Without God, therefore, man is doomed to wander as a nomad, ceaselessly searching for new experiences to fill the gaping vacuum inside. This endless hunt for novelty results both in an unrelenting hunger for new ideas (Acts 17.21), or the urge to acquire more and more new possessions (Ecc. 5.10-11; Luke 12.15). On a more trivial and mundane level it gives rise to a non-stop diet of fashion, fantasy, frivolity and fun. In our own age, an ever-multiplying array of music, TV and social media act as thought-suppressants, concealing the void within, and when these fail to satisfy, we have virtual reality and drugs to numb the pain. The question is not how to face truth, but how to escape from it. It is a wound which, ultimately, cannot be cured (Jer. 51.9).

This also extends to our moral choices. In a 'me-centred' world there are no absolute standards: ancient boundary stones have been removed, morality is relative and extreme tolerance leads to an anarchy of ethical values. 'Everyone does what is right in his own eyes' (Judges 21.25 RSV), but nothing ever really satisfies.

All that we try, in the end, simply leads into greater and greater futility. Having dethroned the Creator who gives meaning and purpose to everything, we find ourselves wandering instead in a maze of pointlessness and hopelessness, seeking desperately to salvage some vestige of meaning from the moral and spiritual vacuum which engulfs us.

How did we get to this point? Let us take a journey through God's long record of dealings with mankind to find out where things went wrong.

Questions to Consider:

(i)   Considering the passage from Philippians 2.5-8, how has Christ's example of self-emptying and servanthood impacted our lives personally? How can we demonstrate that more effectively to those around us on a daily basis?

(ii)   Read the story of the Prodigal Son (Luke 15.11-32). What do you think were the factors that lured him away from his father's house into the arms of the world? What brought him back to his senses, and how might his perspective on life have been changed by his experience?

(iii)   How do the values of the culture around us impact the order of priorities in our lives? Which allurements pose the greatest personal risk of coming between us and God?

2 A TALE OF TWO TREES

According to the Bible, human history begins in a garden not far from the present ruins of Babylon. In the centre of the garden were two trees.

One tree was God's gift and imparted a life of daily dependency on God, an unbroken fellowship with him. This intimate communion can be summed up in two simple words: **'with God'**.

The other tree seemed to offer enlightenment, by offering an independent source of knowledge and wisdom. This alternative path can be summed up in the words **'like God'**.

Behind this choice lay two potential destinies for human history and ultimately two conflicting spiritual kingdoms. All Adam and Eve needed to do to stay on track was to keep listening to the voice of God and keep eating from the tree of life. But, as we know, other forces were at play:

> Now the snake was more crafty than any of the wild animals the LORD God had made. He said to the woman, 'Did God really say, "You must not eat from any tree in the garden"?'

The woman said to the snake, 'We may eat fruit from the trees in the garden, but God did say, "You must not eat fruit from the tree that is in the middle of the garden, and you must not touch it, or you will die."'

'You will not certainly die,' the snake said to the woman. 'For God knows that when you eat from it your eyes will be opened, and you will be **like God**, knowing good and evil.'

When the woman saw that the fruit of the tree was good for food and pleasing to the eye, and also desirable for gaining wisdom, she took some and ate it. She also gave some to her husband, who was with her, and he ate it. Then the eyes of both of them were opened, and they realised that they were naked; so they sewed fig leaves together and made coverings for themselves. (Gen. 3.1-7)

What was it that made the knowledge of good and evil so toxic? Outwardly, the fruit seemed to be attractive enough. The quest for knowledge and wisdom has always been a compelling one. But pursued independently of God this quest becomes an end in itself, leading us not towards the ultimate truth it purports to reveal, but into a trackless waste further and further away from absolute reality.

Not only was the knowledge of goodness delusional without recognising God as its source, but it was ultimately self-destructive: the more they would know about goodness, the more they would know about evil in equal measure.

It seems certain that God would have given Adam and Eve a profound insight into these things in his own time. His desire is for us to have the mind of Christ, in whom *all* God's treasures of wisdom and knowledge are hidden (Col. 2.3). The Bible promises that in the end we will know *all* things (1 Cor. 13.12) even as we are known. But the context is always a relationship with him at the centre.

But sadly our ancestors made the wrong choice. Suddenly they discovered all sorts of things they really did not want to know (Ecc. 1.18). And now God seemed somehow strangely absent from their new mode of being.

One of the things Adam acquired through eating of the fruit was an awareness and focus on himself. Before he ate the fruit Adam was God-conscious, not self-conscious. You could have asked him, 'Tell me about Eve' or 'Tell me about the animals' or 'Tell me about God' and he could have replied in great detail. But had you asked him, 'Tell me about yourself,' you might have encountered a blank expression. It was outside his full range of understanding.

The Bible tells us that when Adam and Eve ate the fruit, 'their eyes were opened.' But as one set of eyes opened, another set of eyes closed. They exchanged a clear view of reality for a distorted one. The restless quest for meaning and identity is a fruit of the 'knowledge of good and evil' in contrast to the 'givenness' of the tree of life.

The end result was that they were forced to look inwards. Suddenly they became narcissistic and preoccupied by self. The meaning of their life was no longer around them but had to be found *within* them.

This raises a profound question of self-worth. Before the fall it was relationship which defined who we are - first and foremost, relationship to God - but also relationship to the earth (the name 'adam' is related to the word for 'earth') and relationship to each other (the name 'woman' in Hebrew is related to the word for 'man').

After the fall, however, identity begins to be defined by *what we do* and not *who we are*. Adam names his wife 'Eve' not because of *who she is* but because of *what she does* (as mother of all the living). Similarly, when their children are introduced, we are immediately told *what they did* (Abel kept flocks, and Cain worked the soil - Genesis 4.2).

The inevitable result was that, further down the line (as we observed in the last chapter) much of humanity would simply become cogs in a machine, an individual being valued solely on what he or she can achieve. Derek Kidner points out, for example, how the Fall gave rise to 'an unbalanced view of marriage' where 'the wife's ultimate *raison d'être* is the production of children ... in effect a means to an end.'[1]

Another consequence of looking inwards is that humanity begins to project its inner turmoil onto the world around, dividing reality into separate compartments. In the case of Adam and Eve, we see them carving up their world into opposing halves - clothed and unclothed, clean and unclean, public and private, sacred and secular - where there had been no such distinction before. The legacy of this for many Christians today is a fatal double-mindedness, as we try to live out two separate and unrelated existences across two spheres.

One result is a preoccupation with the way things look on the outside, as opposed to the inner reality behind them. Deceived by the apparent outward attractiveness of the tree, Adam and Eve become enslaved to superficial appearance and external attraction. What *appears* good becomes more important for them than what *is* good.

Unlike Jesus, who 'had no beauty or majesty to attract us to him, nothing in his appearance that we should desire him', the need to save face and to *look* good on the outside becomes paramount. And this is where an element of subterfuge creeps in. Realising that they are naked, the first response of Adam and Eve is to manufacture clothes, but with the aim of *concealing something defensively.* Undue preoccupation with external appearance is ultimately about hiding the truth.

This is a step of huge significance. Before eating from the fruit of the tree Adam and Eve were 'naked and unashamed': they were 'walking in the light', and living in a state of transparency and openness. Now their actions became furtive, secretive and evasive. Babylon is portrayed in Revelation as a 'mystery' - concealing hidden truths. Secrecy, encryption and disguise are the watchwords of our modern age.

The price of becoming *like* God was that they were no longer *with* God. The result of being *self*-centred and *self*-defined was a fragmentation. Unity with God was broken. Unity between sexes was broken. Unity between people was broken. Unity with nature was broken. The inner unity of self was broken.

The heart cry of the human soul is for this unity to be restored. The first appearance of Babylon in the Bible was the attempt to establish this unity by artificial means through the tower of Babel. Ultimately religion and secularism spring from the same root of wanting to create this ourselves through human effort.

They are attempting to do what, in fact, only God can do. True unity will only come when heaven and earth themselves come together in Christ. Attempts to unify by any other means ultimately backfire and only generate more brokenness. The end result, as we see with Babel, is simply fragmentation and confusion.

In the end, the direction of travel was wrong. As we read in Genesis chapter 11, Babel's premature attempt to unify mankind by thrusting *upwards* was only halted by God *going down* to earth to call a halt. Over and over again, religion has attempted to scale more heights, but in the incarnation God *comes down* as one of us. At Pentecost, when Babel was finally put into reverse, the God *descended* through his Spirit and wove together a single message from the apparent confusion of languages. And in the triumphant closing pages of the Bible it is the New Jerusalem which *descends* from heaven, to reunite humanity with the God who ever since that first transgression has longed to walk in our midst once more.

The simple truth is that there is no ladder we can build into heaven. The only way we can enter is to be born *from above* (the literal meaning of John 3.3). It is entirely God's initiative to which we can add nothing of our own, other than a complete surrender of our will into his.

This is apparent in the parable of two gates which Jesus told. The narrow, unpromising gate is actually the one that leads to life. But the wide gate seems much easier and far more inviting. Like the tree of knowledge, it looks good on the outside, but it is a trap.

There is a way that appears to be right, but in the end it leads to death.' (Prov. 14.12)

Questions to Consider:

(i)   Are we tempted to hide from God when we make mistakes? How can we encourage ourselves to keep our eyes fixed on Jesus in all circumstances, rather than turning in on ourselves?

(ii)   Compare the accounts of Eve in the Garden of Eden with Mary Magdalene after the Resurrection (Gen. 3.1-20; John 20.10-18). What are the similarities between the two stories, and how does the second one turn the first on its head? Have we ever, like Mary, encountered Christ at a time when we least expected him? (Consider also Matthew 25.37-40 and Luke 24.30-31).

(iii)   What broken or strained relationships are there between ourselves and those around us? How might this disfigure the kingdom of God in our lives? What steps can we take to put things right?

3 A TALE OF TWO WOMEN

> This is what the LORD says: "Stand at the crossroads and look; ask for the ancient paths, ask where the good way is, and walk in it, and you will find rest for your souls.'
>
> (Jer. 6.16)

At many points in our life we arrive at a junction. We have a genuine choice to make, and our future is pulled in two directions. Sadly, without learning to be still and taking time to study God's word and to seek God's heart, we can all too often head off towards disaster.

We have already seen how in the Garden of Eden Adam and Eve arrive at such a crossroads. As we know, they took a tragic wrong turning which unleashed endless repercussions for us all.

However, the same kind of challenge appears again and again throughout history. It is expressed in different ways and using different imagery throughout scripture. In Proverbs, for example, we find the choice expressed in the words of two very different invitations:

Wisdom has built her house;
    she has set up its seven pillars.
She has prepared her meat and mixed her wine;
    she has also set her table.
She has sent out her servants, and she calls
    from the highest point of the city,

    "Let all who are simple come to my house!"
To those who have no sense she says,
    "Come, eat my food
    and drink the wine I have mixed.
Leave your simple ways and you will live;
    walk in the way of insight." (9.1-6)

Folly is an unruly woman;
    she is simple and knows nothing.
She sits at the door of her house,
    on a seat at the highest point of the city,
calling out to those who pass by,
    who go straight on their way,
    "Let all who are simple come to my house!"
To those who have no sense she says,
    "Stolen water is sweet;
    food eaten in secret is delicious!"
But little do they know that the dead are there,
    that her guests are deep in the realm of the dead. (9.13-18)

It is not difficult to see the parallels here with the two trees in Genesis. Both represent two goals and two kingdoms. Both are occupying the same location, the trees at the centre of the garden and the women at the highest point of the city. Both are offering something to eat that is life-transforming, for good or for bad. And in both cases, the choice is the same: one is open and above board, the other entices with secrecy; one speaks truth while the other lures by deception. One leads to life; the other leads to death.

Earlier in Proverbs the contrast between the two invitations is even more stark. On the one hand the fruits of divine wisdom are shown to exceed anything this world can offer, and, in a direct link to Genesis, nothing less than a 'tree of life':

> Blessed are those who find wisdom,
>   those who gain understanding,
> for she is more profitable than silver
>   and yields better returns than gold.
> She is more precious than rubies;
>   nothing you desire can compare with her.
> Long life is in her right hand;
>   in her left hand are riches and honour.
> Her ways are pleasant ways,
>   and all her paths are peace.
> She is a *tree of life* to those who take hold of her;
>   those who hold her fast will be blessed. (3.13-18)

Folly, meanwhile, is presented as an adulteress, with a hidden agenda (7.10) that leads its unsuspecting victims into a deadly trap:

> Wisdom will save you also from the adulterous woman,
>   from the wayward woman with her seductive words,
> who has left the partner of her youth
>   and ignored the covenant she made before God.
> Surely her house leads down to death
>   and her paths to the spirits of the dead.
> None who go to her return
>   or attain the paths of life. (2.16-19)

In a sense, the Bible is like a great symphony, relentlessly exploring the conflict between these two opposing themes. While God's original vision wins through triumphantly in the final pages of scripture, the pull in the opposite direction remains strong and restless almost to the end.

One small example of this pull appears in Zechariah chapter 5, where the 'adulteress' theme that we see in Proverbs is developed a little further. Here we are presented with the image of a woman whose name is 'Wickedness', who is concealed in a basket (a hint at the secrecy motif once more) and is being transported through the air to Shinar, where a house is being prepared for her. The location is significant, since this is an ancient name for Babylonia.

This is an intriguing pointer to another conflict between two rival women in the second part of Isaiah, with Babylon being personified on one hand and Jerusalem on the other. While these symbolic figures do not correspond exactly with the two women portrayed in Proverbs, they might be said to represent opposite human responses to the two invitations that Proverbs throws open.

Of the two women in Isaiah, it is Jerusalem (Zion) who receives by far the greatest emphasis. She is down in the dust, but will be clothed in beautiful garments (52.1-2); she is desolate and ashamed, but will be exalted over the nations (49.13-23); she is afflicted, but will be comforted (51.21-23; 54.7-8); she is a widow, but will be married (54.4-5); she is barren, but will receive many children in a single day (54.1; 66.8-9).

Babylon, by contrast, is almost a direct reversal of this. She is enthroned like a queen, but will end naked in the dust (47.1-2,7); she is exalted over the nations, but will be desolate and ashamed (47.5-11); she lives in comfort, but will be afflicted (47.8,11); she says she will never know widowhood or the loss of children, but receives both in a single day (47.8-9).

In Revelation, where the symphony reaches its final climax, these descriptions of Babylon and the New Jerusalem are worked out in even more vivid terms. One is a prostitute, the other is a bride (17.1,5; 21.2,9); one is a habitation for demons, the other is closed to anything unclean (18.2; 21.27); one has sins piled up to heaven, the other comes *down* from heaven, untainted by sin (18.5; 21.10-11). One faces nothing but death, mourning and famine; in the other, these things are abolished for ever (18.8; 21.4).

As in Proverbs, these two competing themes represent two fundamental destinies, life and blessing on the one hand, and humiliation and death on the other. And as in Genesis they offer the possibility of being 'with God' for ever (Is. 54.10; Rev. 21.3) or simply 'like God' (Is. 47.8,10; Rev. 18.7). Moreover, as with both passages, they offer a contrast between walking in the light (Is. 60.1-3, 19-20; Rev. 21.23-4) or hiding in secrecy and darkness (Is. 47.10; Rev. 17.5).

It is in particular this desire to be *like* God, to usurp his place, which seems to stand out most strongly in both the Isaiah and Revelation accounts:

> 'You said, "**I** am for ever –
>   the eternal queen!" …
> 'Now then, listen, you lover of pleasure,
>   lounging in your security
> and saying to yourself,
>   "**I** am, and there is none besides me" ' (Is. 47.7-8)

> 'In her heart she boasts,
>   "**I** sit enthroned as queen.
> **I** am not a widow;
>   **I** will never mourn." ' (Rev. 18.7)

Such bold self-advancement stands in direct opposition to the life-giving 'I am' statements of Christ. As we have seen, it is only centred around Christ's self-humbling on the cross (Phil. 2.5-11) that humanity can attain its true God-given destiny. And whereas the church has already been raised to heavenly places in Christ Jesus (Eph. 2.6), the end result for Babylon is the opposite.

The 'me'-centred pattern should be familiar by now: it echoes the repeated 'I will' declarations of the king of Babylon from Isaiah 14 that we considered in Chapter One. Indeed, Nebuchadnezzar's own words, still preserved in the ruins of Babylon, sound remarkably close in character:

> **I** have completed its magnificence with silver, gold, other metals, stone, enamelled bricks, fir, and pine. ... **I** built and finished it. **I** have highly exalted its head with bricks covered with copper ... **I** undertook to build porticoes around the crude brick masses, and the casings of burnt bricks. **I** adapted the circuits, **I** put the inscription of my name in the kitir of the portico. **I** set my hand to finish it, and to exalt its head. As it had been in ancient days, so **I** exalted its summit.[1]

Similar in tone is Nebuchadnezzar's prayer to Marduk, recorded on a tablet in the British Museum in London, where he asks:

> 'May the temple **I** have built endure for all time and may **I** be satisfied with its splendour; in its midst may **I** attain old age, may **I** be sated with offspring; therein may **I** receive the heavy tribute of all mankind; from the horizon of heaven to the zenith, may **I** have no enemies; may my descendants live therein forever and rule over the people.'[2]

Likewise, the account of Nebuchadnezzar in Daniel chapter 4 reveals an almost identical frame of mind to the passages we have just quoted:

> Twelve months later, as the king was walking on the roof of the royal palace of Babylon, he said, 'Is not this the great Babylon **I** have built as the royal residence, by **my** mighty power and for the glory of **my** majesty?'

The instant response from heaven is devastating:

'This is what is decreed for you, King Nebuchadnezzar: Your royal authority has been taken from you. You will be driven away from people and will live with the wild animals; you will eat grass like the ox. Seven times will pass by for you until you acknowledge that the Most High is sovereign over all kingdoms on earth and gives them to anyone he wishes.'

Immediately what had been said about Nebuchadnezzar was fulfilled. He was driven away from people and ate grass like the ox. His body was drenched with the dew of heaven until his hair grew like the feathers of an eagle and his nails like the claws of a bird. (Dan. 4.29-33)

Historians have often questioned the veracity of Daniel's account, and yet it bears all the hallmarks of a very rare medical condition called 'boanthropy'. Persian tradition records that the prince Majd al-Dawla was cured by the famous physician Avicenna (980-1037 AD) of the delusion that he was a cow.[3] The Old Testament scholar Roland Harrison also comments on another clinical case in a psychiatric institution in 1946, which bears an uncanny resemblance to that of Nebuchadnezzar:

His mental symptoms included pronounced anti-social tendencies, and because of this he spent the entire day from dawn to dusk outdoors, in the grounds of the institution ... it was his custom to pluck up and eat handfuls of the grass as he went along. ... The writer was able to examine him cursorily, and the only physical abnormality noted consisted of a lengthening of the hair and a coarse, thickened condition of the fingernails.[4]

However humiliating this might have been (and contemporary records of the time may hint at just such a bout of mental illness)[5] the king's ultimate fate was infinitely worse, as Isaiah records:

> The realm of the dead below is all astir
>> to meet you at your coming;
> it rouses the spirits of the departed to greet you—
>> all those who were leaders in the world;
> it makes them rise from their thrones—
>> all those who were kings over the nations.
> They will all respond,
>> they will say to you,
> 'You also have become weak, as we are;
>> you have become like us.'
> All your pomp has been brought down to the grave,
>> along with the noise of your harps;
> maggots are spread out beneath you
>> and worms cover you. (Is. 14.9-11)

It is clear, however, that God's warnings about complacency and arrogance extend far beyond the remit of specific individuals. In the previous chapter of Isaiah, Babylon becomes a symbol for a mindset which is national or even worldwide in its scope:

> See, the day of the LORD is coming
>> – a cruel day, with wrath and fierce anger –
> to make the land [of Babylon] desolate
>> and destroy the sinners within it.
> The stars of heaven and their constellations
>> will not show their light.
> The rising sun will be darkened
>> and the moon will not give its light.
> I will punish the world for its evil,
>> the wicked for their sins.
> I will put an end to the arrogance of the haughty
>> and will humble the pride of the ruthless. (Is. 13.9-11)

Similarly, in Jeremiah, we see the judgement on Babylon extends beyond the man at the helm to fall on the entire nation itself:

> 'I am against you, you destroying mountain,
>> you who destroy the whole earth,'

declares the LORD.
'I will stretch out my hand against you,
     roll you off the cliffs,
     and make you a burnt-out mountain.' (Jer. 51.25)

'Even if Babylon ascends to the heavens
     and fortifies her lofty stronghold,
     I will send destroyers against her,'
declares the LORD.   (Jer. 51.53)

In God's economy, therefore, there is only one way to go up - and that is to go down! Or, as Jesus explained,

'You know that the rulers of the Gentiles lord it over them, and their high officials exercise authority over them. Not so with you. Instead, whoever wants to become great among you must be your servant, and whoever wants to be first must be your slave—just as the Son of Man did not come to be served, but to serve, and to give his life as a ransom for many.'
(Matt. 20.25-28)

The voice of Wisdom never stops calling out to us, and yet so often, to our own downfall, we choose to ignore and carry on in our own way. There is a universal warning here to all of us, therefore, not just to the great and the mighty. *Whoever* raises himself will be humbled.

Questions to Consider:

(i)   What are the major choices that we have made in our lives and what factors guided us in reaching those decisions? How can we fully discern God's will for the choices that lie ahead?

(ii)   Read Matthew 4.1-10. How might the temptations that Jesus faced relate to the ones that we encounter in our everyday situations? How did he overcome them, and what can we learn from his experience?

(iii)   What are the 'me' factors in our lives that cause us to put self on the throne? How can we change the dynamic and allow God to take the driving seat in our lives on a permanent basis?

4 THE EMPEROR'S NEW CLOTHES

Genesis is the book of beginnings. As we have seen, human destiny starts in such a promising way. The earth has been ordered from its initial watery chaos, the animals have been brought together to be named, and a precious human couple are tending the garden in obedience and fellowship with God, living in a state of blissful innocence.

Soon, however, events take a different turn. Tempted to taste the forbidden fruit, the couple become aware that they are naked and separated from God. The result of their actions is a curse that extends to the entire human race.

If we jump forward a few chapters to the aftermath of the Flood we encounter a strikingly similar scene. The land has once more emerged from another watery chaos, the animals have been saved, a precious human remnant rescued, and the beauty of human fellowship with God is beginning to be established afresh through one man's act of obedience.

But soon things begin to unravel yet again after Noah and his family leave the Ark. Tempted in a vineyard where the grapes have fermented, Noah becomes drunk.

The end results prove catastrophic for generations to come. Noah's son Ham looks irreverently on his father naked and helpless and apparently mocks him, resulting in Noah cursing an important branch of Ham's family line when he awakes.

At first sight this looks like a simple lesson in the dangers of over-indulgence. Certainly eating the wrong kind of fruit causes a lot of problems in Genesis!

Yet thousands of years later these two descriptions of nakedness are re-framed in completely new terms. The pathway of human history jumps forward to a rough wooden cross and yet another naked man, upon whom all God's plans meet once more.

The cross throws a fresh light on the drama of the Garden of Eden. A second Adam has arrived on the scene who is punished for all the sins of the first Adam. Unlike his distant human ancestor, however, Jesus does not seek to conceal his nakedness. He offers no resistance when he is stripped, humiliated and tortured in the most brutal way imaginable. He is naked to the world and naked to the powers of darkness. He endured the shame of our nakedness that we should be clothed with the glory of his righteousness.

The cross also throws a fresh light on the life of Noah. On that cross, drinking the 'cup' of God's judgement, Jesus finds himself naked, exposed, humiliated and mocked, as Noah had been. Like Noah, he is dishonoured by his own flesh and blood, those he came to save.

There is an important point of contrast, therefore, between the two Genesis accounts. The story of Adam and Eve vividly describes the shame of sin, and our sense of nakedness before God. The story of Noah and Ham, on the other hand, might remind us of God's nakedness before us, as revealed in the cross of Christ, when he took our shame and inadequacy upon himself.

This is apparent in the striking parallels between the experience of Noah and that of Jesus. If the interpretation of the passage given by the Jewish historian Flavius Josephus is correct, Ham wants to look 'cool' in front of his brothers by mocking and dishonouring his naked father (*Antiquities of the Jews*, 1.6.3).[1] Thankfully, Noah's two other sons, Shem and Japheth, rejecting their brother's brazenly disrespectful attitude, seek to cover their father's body in a dignified manner:

> But Shem and Japheth took a garment and laid it across their shoulders; then they walked in backwards and covered their father's naked body. Their faces were turned the other way so that they would not see their father naked. (Gen. 9.23)

Jumping ahead to Golgotha we see the same underlying drama played out. On the one hand the Jewish religious leaders make themselves feel smugly superior as they deride the spectacle of a naked preacher on a cross:

> 'He saved others,' they said, 'but he can't save himself! He's the king of Israel! Let him come down now from the cross, and we will believe in him. He trusts in God. Let God rescue him now if he wants him, for he said, "I am the Son of God." ' (Matt. 27.42-43)

In sharp contrast, Nicodemus and Joseph of Arimathea, appalled by the actions of the religious elite, respectfully wrap the (now dead) body of Jesus in strips of linen cloth (John 19.38-40).

Ham's attitude is one we might easily recognise today: arrogant, insolent and totally lacking in respect. For him Noah is a 'loser', an embarrassment, the ultimate in being 'uncool'. By his trying to joke about his father with his brothers, he tries to make himself look smartly superior.

33

In fact, the very outcome that he most fears, the loss of prestige and significance, becomes his destiny (compare Habakkuk 2.15-16). He fails to understand the divine principle that our descendants are blessed only to the degree to which we ourselves have honoured our parents. Like Adam and Eve, he knows he has to live with the consequences and has to look for some way to 'cover up' his mistake.

It is surely no coincidence, then, that it is Ham's grandson, Nimrod, who is the architect of Babylon. The very trends that propel city living forward - the cult of innovation, the undermining of reverence for tribal authority and tradition so ingrained in rural culture - become its driving force. Left unchecked, city life can become focused around the aspirations of the young, in contrast to the centrality of the elderly in traditional cultures. Whereas such rural cultures are always looking backwards, the most ambitious cities have been driven forward by a relentless pursuit of the new (Acts 17.21). In modern society scientists, researchers and inventors, the circumnavigators of new realms of knowledge, have become today's priesthood and the pursuit of knowledge has become a god in its own right.

Urban culture at its most extreme becomes defined by innovation, and a constant debunking of the old. The desire to entertain and impress becomes paramount. It was far more 'cool' for the emperor Nero to burn Christians as human torches for his night-time festivities than to listen to the preachers of the gospel. Actions become justified on the basis of whether they are slick and entertaining rather than through any sense of right and wrong.

Indeed, history shows that, generally, Babylon and its spiritual successors have no respect for the things of God. The Hebrew concept of a personal, universal God is seen as foolishness.

The book of Acts shows that when Paul talked about of the resurrection in Athens, some of his audience sneered (17.32). It was as risible and embarrassing to the privileged élite of the time as it is now within the hallowed precincts of modern academia. To the 'cool' student body on university campuses today, Christians with their strange beliefs and antiquated moral code can appear to be as much a laughing stock as they are to the 'uncool' lecturers who teach them.

Then, as now, exclusivist religion is portrayed as fanatical, anti-progressive, illiberal, and irrational. Acts 26.24 shows us how religion is regarded as superstition by the 'educated' minds of the world:

> At this point Festus interrupted Paul's defence. 'You are out of your mind, Paul!' he shouted. 'Your great learning is driving you insane.'

For us today it can be very tempting to dilute the message of the gospel out of fear of appearing outdated and irrelevant to the modern world. Rather than standing our ground, we may attempt to water down 'hard truths' to make them more palatable to the culture around us. Like Adam and Eve, it is easy to become ashamed of our nakedness and to attempt to make ourselves look 'cool' in the world's eyes by resorting to slick gimmicks or catchy entertainment.

Yet by softening the message of sin, judgement and the cross to provide an easy 'fast-track' access into the kingdom of God we can actually present a false gospel. Jesus warned us that there is no 'wide gate' into the kingdom of heaven - only a narrow one. Recasting Christianity on worldly lines is like putting on fig leaves. Whether we are preaching good works, success, prosperity, or personal fulfilment, we are simply presenting 'filthy rags' in God's sight (Isaiah 64.6) if we are trying to bypass the humiliation of the cross, which is ultimately foolishness to the world.

God's message to us, as it was to Joshua the high priest, is to take off those filthy robes (Zech. 3.4). He has something better for us, just as he had something better for Adam and Eve when he took away their fig-leaves and provided instead the skins of a slaughtered animal, pointing forward to the blood sacrifice of Jesus.

The challenge is whether we might have come to enjoy our fig-leaves too much to want to remove them. Like the Laodiceans, we cry out, 'I am rich; I have acquired wealth and do not need a thing.' But in fact we do not realize that we are 'wretched, pitiful, poor, blind and naked' (Rev 3.17). God warns us, as he warns Babylon in Isaiah 47.3, that 'your nakedness will be exposed and your shame uncovered'.

If God found Adam and Eve unprepared when he returned to walk in the cool of the evening, will we too be caught out when Jesus returns to judge the whole earth? As believers there is a clear warning for us to be ready for when that day comes, as it surely will soon.

The bride in the Song of Solomon has been transported with delight by her beloved, but when she fails to be ready for her lover at the appointed time she is stripped of her robe by her enemies (Song 5.2-7). Her nakedness is the direct consequence of unpreparedness.

For the man in a linen shroud in Mark's gospel (possibly Mark himself), the story is similar. He has just celebrated a Passover supper with Jesus in Jerusalem and heard one of the most powerful sermons it would ever be possible to hear. Like the twelve, he has recklessly promised never to abandon his master. Yet just hours later, he is doing that very thing, deserting Jesus at his time of greatest need in the Garden of Gethsemane in order to avoid capture. The soldiers seize the shroud and he has to escape naked. His nakedness is the direct consequence of running away (Mark 14.51-52).

It is perhaps to these passages that Jesus is referring when he warns us:

> 'Behold, I am coming like a thief! Blessed is the one who stays awake, keeping his garments on, that he may not go about naked and be seen exposed!' (Rev. 16.15 ESV)

What matters is not how we seem in the world's eyes, but how we appear in the eyes of God. Let us not be found naked before him as a church by abandoning the foolishness of the message of Calvary. God himself has stooped down to share in our nakedness (Micah 1.8) clothing himself with our shame in Christ's body on the cross. Let us, then, go to him outside the camp, bearing the disgrace he bore (Heb. 13.13). No price can be too great for the one who experienced abject humiliation, mockery and torture for our sakes, in order that our shame might be transfigured into his incomparable glory.

Questions to Consider:

(i)   How do we react when others mock us and despise us? What examples from scripture could help us cope better in such situations?

(ii)   Read Mark 14.66-72. What factors led Peter to deny Jesus three times in a row? How would he have felt afterwards? Would we have reacted any differently? What changed him later in life?

(iii) Under what circumstances are we slow to respond to God's beckoning, or deliberately run away from his call to make a stand for Christ? Are we dominated by a fear of what other people might think of us, and, if so, what would it take to overcome this?

5 FROM ABEL TO BABEL

Inside all of us is a deep yearning. As we saw earlier, we have been created with 'eternity in our hearts' - the longing for the New Jerusalem, where we are fully reunited as family with God, our eternal loving father. Abraham and his faithful forebears looked ahead to a city built by God (Heb. 11.13-16).

Just as Adam and Eve were incomplete without each other, so humanity, as the prospective bride of Christ, is incomplete without him. We are longing, as Paul reminds us, to be 'clothed with our heavenly dwelling' (2 Cor. 5.2).

As we saw in the last chapter, however, just as Adam and Eve attempted to 'make do' with fig leaves in Genesis chapter 3 to cover their nakedness, so we in turn try and compensate for the spiritual void within through our own ingenuity. The mistake they made, and the one we continue to make today, as followers of any religion or none, is our failure to see the need for a blood sacrifice. We noticed that while they thought that they could solve the problem through their own efforts, God clothed them with the skins of an animal whose blood had been shed.

Cain makes the same mistake in the next chapter of Genesis with tragic consequences. He believes, mistakenly, that he can win God's favour through his own labours. Because the land had been cursed, his offering was produced through 'painful toil' and 'the sweat of his brow' (3.17,19). Abel, by contrast, realises that only a blood sacrifice is sufficient for him to maintain fellowship with God.

In the background we can see that Cain suffers from a fatal flaw - a poor self-image. Like his parents with their hastily-sewn fig-leaves, this damaged sense of self-worth drives him to attempt putting himself right before God through human effort alone. It is this insecurity, erupting to the surface in a torrent of anger when he sees his offering has been rejected, that causes him to murder his brother out of sheer envy. Out of the same root of insecurity and vulnerability he then asks the Lord for a protective mark.

It is Cain, not his brother Seth, who goes on to build the first city mentioned in the Bible (Gen. 4.17). Forced otherwise to wander the land in a rootless existence, the city (though probably just a hamlet by today's standards) offered a sanctuary and a protective retreat from a hostile environment. By creating a legacy for Cain, it helps him to mask his own poor self-image and perhaps erase the memory of his blood-guilt.

Alec Motyer comments that

> Cain has to be responsible ... for his own security: the building of the city is the outward and visible sign of the self-sufficient man - but also of the reclusive man: Adam hid himself behind fig-leaves; Cain behind stone walls.[1]

Like the improvised garments of Adam and Eve, therefore, the function of the first city was initially defensive - to cover exposure and vulnerability - a retreat from God and from the natural order. In keeping the capriciousness of nature at arms' length, it offered a measure of protection from wild animals and the ravages of the elements. It marks another step away from dependency to 'self-sufficiency'.

Cain's descendants went on to develop crafts such as metal-working which made it possible for them to make a living that did not depend on tilling the soil. These emergent craftsmen and traders enabled cities to grow and to establish greater independence from the land. The result was yet another move further from direct dependence on God, the provider of rain, seasons and fruitfulness.

And yet behind this remains a fundamental sense of insecurity and wounded pride. Lamech tells his wives:

> I have killed a man for wounding me,
>   a young man for injuring me.
> If Cain is avenged seven times,
>   then Lamech seventy-seven times. (Gen. 4.23-24)

There is a hint here, perhaps, of the deadly use to which metal tools would be used, as weapons of human conflict. Warfare has a long and tragic history, but it is perhaps significant that the first mention of it in the Bible later involves the king of Babylon (Shinar) himself (Gen. 14.8-12). From the frustration and low self-worth of Cain and his descendants the roots of genocide are born.

Noah was also a builder, but he created *in response* to what God was telling him. Instead of insecurity, we see an extraordinary level of trust in God despite the outward circumstances. Not only was he willing to endure the mirth and contempt of those around him by constructing a huge ship in a completely landlocked place, but also had to cope with the inevitable reactions of his family who were hauled on board the ark for a whole week before a single drop of rain had fallen!

By contrast Nimrod, Noah's great-grandson, was a very different character. The name 'Nimrod' may relate to a root which means 'we rebel'. Like Cain, he appears to have begun as a wandering nomad - 'a mighty hunter before the LORD'. Genesis 10.10-12 suggests that he went on to establish a series of cities. One of them, Calah, still bears his name today – Nimrud – and for a time was the capital of Assyria.

His first project, however, seems to have been Babel. As we have seen, he and his co-workers wanted to 'make a name for themselves' by building a tower reaching to the heavens. Given that there was little stone in Babylonia but much clay, bricks became the ideal building material. Technology, even in this primitive form, became the driver of this upward vision. Ingenuity so often degenerates into idolatry.

Their statement 'Let us build ...', by echoing the very words of God himself in Genesis 1.26 ('Let us make ...') is telling. In attempting to compete with God or perhaps even replace him, it fulfilled the serpent's invitation for us to be *like* God rather than achieving our ultimate purpose, to be *with* God, which we see fulfilled in Babylon's antithesis, the New Jerusalem. This attempt to supplant God becomes a continuing preoccupation for Babylon, as we have already seen in the bold claims we find in Isaiah: 'I will make myself like the Most High' (Is. 14.14) and 'I am, and there is none besides me' (Is. 47.8, 10).

There is no record in scripture of how high the tower was, but the 1st century BC *Book of Jubilees* mentions the tower's height as being 5,433 cubits and 2 palms.[2] Not only would this, in modern terms, have been over a mile and a half high, but later Jewish legends even multiplied this exponentially by describing a whole year's journey for the last builder to get his final hod of bricks to the top![3]

In his *Antiquities of the Jews* (1.4.2) the Jewish writer Flavius Josephus offers several intriguing extra details about Babel. Firstly, he writes that Nimrod changed the government into a form of tyranny so that the people might rely on him and not on God. Secondly, he suggests that the tower was an attempt to escape another divine judgement through a flood (its materials - burnt brick cemented with mortar made from bitumen - were deliberately designed to be waterproof). And thirdly, he argues that it was Nimrod's personal act of revenge on God for destroying humanity through the deluge, a theme that reappears in a number of later Jewish writings, including the Talmud.[4]

As with Cain, therefore, the motivation was similar: there was an outward show of defiance and pride, but the underlying root was a sense of fear and vulnerability. To this very day man thinks he can outsmart God, but he never succeeds. Voltaire famously tried to debunk the Christian faith, but after his death his home became the headquarters of the French Bible Society.

History is littered with schemes to usurp the place of God. Babel was the first attempt at one plan, one language, one network, one city, and one global power-base. While all these things are to be characteristics of the New Jerusalem, when they spring from man they are doomed to fail. The 'oneness' is an attempt to create a rival system to that of the kingdom of God - just like the arrogant presumption of the 'let us build' declaration. The only true template of unity is the true church as pictured in the New Testament, and, as we saw earlier, this is built on a reversal of Babylonian principles.

Far from creating the unity it was designed to achieve, therefore, Babel backfired. There was confusion, division and misunderstanding. In Babel, just as in Eden, God describes his action in demolishing the counter-kingdom set up against him *in the plural*: 'Let *us* go down and confuse their language' (v.7 - compare his use of the plural in Genesis 3.22 after man's first rebellion). He sets the whole weight of the Trinity against man's premature attempt at unity. By scattering languages and driving people away from one another, he forced them to fulfil his original purpose, which was that man should fill the earth and subdue it.

James Frazer, in his book *Folklore in the Old Testament*, points out a number of stories from all around the world with conspicuous similarities to the Babel account. Among the ancient inhabitants of Mexico, for example (a land with many ancient ziggurats of its own) we find a story of giants who built a tower to reach the sky. The Lord of the Heavens, aroused to fury, summoned the inhabitants of the sky to destroy the tower and scatter its inhabitants. Another story in Mexico records that after a great flood, people gathered together to build a tower to protect themselves from any future deluge. However, after their languages were confused, they went on to populate different parts of the earth.[5]

The inhabitants of the Admiralty Islands, to the north of New Guinea, also recounted an ancient attempt to create buildings reaching up to heaven, resulting in confusion between different languages. Likewise the Karen people of Burma record that their ancestors moved there after a great pagoda was abandoned thirty generations after the first man, when the single language of the world was thrown into disarray.[6]

Furthermore, a fragmentary text on an Assyrian tablet from Nineveh, now held in the British Museum in London, seems to record the same event:

Of him, his heart was evil,
[…] against the father of all the gods was wicked,
[…] of him, his heart was evil,
[…] Babylon brought to subjection,
[small] and great **he confounded their speech**.
Their strong place (tower) all the day they founded;
to their strong place in the night
entirely he made an end.
In his anger also word thus he poured out:
[to] scatter abroad he set his face
he gave this? command, their counsel was confused.[7]

Even if the Babel story ended in chaos, however, this was certainly not the end for Babylon or the dream which underpinned it. In the 17th century BC Hammurabi (1792-1750 BC) had Babylon redesigned, heightening its walls, and introducing a grid-like network of wide, straight streets that were paved with bricks and bitumen, lined with impressive buildings and interlaced with canals. At its peak it became the first city in the world whose population reached more than 200,000 people. Through diplomacy and military conquest he united Mesopotamia under Babylonian rule, establishing a single administrative and legal system and a common language.

Nebuchadnezzar II (604-561 BC) was even more ambitious. Under his rulership Babylon was rebuilt as a perfect square, 120 stadia in length on each side, an extraordinary anticipation of the measurements of the New Jerusalem (12,000 stadia in each side). The Greek historian Herodotus, who lived just over a century later, commented that 'in magnificence there is no other city that approaches to it'.[8] The hanging gardens, so elaborate that they used machinery to water them, were counted among the seven wonders of the ancient world. Nebuchadnezzar also included what may have been the world's first public museum.

Most importantly, he attempted to rebuild the tower of Babel. His own words about the project seem to contain a significant recollection of the original tower and God's judgement upon it:

> The tower, the eternal house, which I founded and built. I have completed its magnificence with silver, gold, other metals, stone, enamelled bricks, fir and pine. The first, which is the house of the earth's base, the most ancient monument of Babylon; I built and finished it. ... **A former king built it, they reckon 42 ages, but he did not complete its head. Since a remote time people had abandoned it, without order expressing their words. Since that time the earthquake and the thunder had dispersed the sun-dried clay. The bricks of the casing had been split, and the earth of the interior had been scattered in heaps.** ... As it had been in ancient days, so I exalted its summit.[9]

Herodotus described Nebuchadnezzar's structure as follows:

> In the middle of the precinct there was a tower of solid masonry, a furlong in length and breadth, upon which was raised a second tower, and on that a third, and so on up to eight. The ascent to the top is on the outside, by a path which winds round all the towers. When one is about half-way up, one finds a resting-place and seats, where persons are wont to sit some time on their way to the summit. On the topmost tower there is a spacious temple, and inside the temple stands a couch of unusual size, richly adorned, with a golden table by its side. There is no statue of any kind set up in the place, nor is the chamber occupied of nights by any one but a single native woman, who, as the Chaldaeans, the priests of this god, affirm, is chosen for himself by the deity out of all the women of the land.[10]

Few men in history ever achieved the eminence and notoriety of Nebuchadnezzar. One of his greatest successors, Alexander the Great, who finished his short but remarkable life in Babylon in 323 BC, had the tower demolished, planning to build an even greater one, but never lived to see it through. It ended its life as nothing but a heap of rubble.

And this is the fate, ultimately, that met Babylon itself, just as Jeremiah had promised hundreds of years beforehand.

> Because of the LORD's anger she will not be inhabited but will be completely desolate. All who pass Babylon will be appalled; they will scoff because of all her wounds. (50.13)

> Babylon will be a heap of ruins, a haunt of jackals, an object of horror and scorn, a place where no one lives. (51.37)

> Then say, 'So will Babylon sink to rise no more because of the disaster I will bring on her. And her people will fall.' (51.64)

But in that case, we are left with something of a conundrum. Why does Revelation continue to present Babylon as a living reality long after it was destroyed? Why does Peter end his first letter by describing himself 'in Babylon', a city that by his time had long disappeared? It is now time to move on from the quiet reflections of our opening chapters and grapple on a more objective level with some serious lessons of history, as we begin to answer this question.

Questions to Consider:

(i)   What insecurities in our lives cause us to retreat behind protective walls? Is such a response inevitable, or is there a different way in which we could respond?

(ii)   Read 2 Samuel 24.15-25. What was the effect of the blood sacrifice on the plague on Israel? How might we apply this when praying in a time of disaster or crisis? (See Hebrews 9.22 and Revelation 12.11). Why is the blood of Jesus the ultimate antidote to the power of sin and Satan?

(iii)   What are the towers we are attempting to build in our lives? Are we constructing on solid foundations and with materials that will endure the test of God's judgement (Matt. 7.24-27; 1 Cor. 3.10-15) or merely raising up a temporary folly to our own vanity?

6 THE DREAM THAT UNLOCKS HISTORY

One of the abiding images of the early years of the twenty-first century was the toppling of a huge statue of Saddam Hussein in Baghdad. It offered a momentary window of hope for a better future - hope that was sadly dashed by the maelstrom of chaos that followed in its wake.

Saddam saw himself in part as a successor to Nebuchadnezzar, the powerful king of Babylon whom we have discussed in previous chapters. At the entrance to the ruins of Babylon he placed a portrait of himself standing with Nebuchadnezzar and had inscriptions bearing his name put on many individual bricks, as his illustrious forebear had done, describing himself as the 'son of Nebuchadnezzar'.

Nebuchadnezzar, it may be remembered, also built a great statue in the plains of Babylonia and it was their refusal to worship it that landed Shadrach, Meshach and Abednego in the fiery furnace.

Statues do not get a good press in the Bible. They are almost always associated with arrogance, idolatry and emperor worship. Saul's desire to set up a monument to himself is one of the first marks of his demise as king of Israel (1 Sam. 15.12).

One statue, however, carries a particularly significant role in scripture, even though in physical terms never existed at all. It originates in a terrifying dream which King Nebuchadnezzar has earlier in his reign (Dan. 2.1). Summoning all his magicians and astrologers, he threatens them with imminent execution unless they can tell him what he saw. In desperation they turn to the Hebrew exile Daniel, who, doubtless to their enormous relief, is able to explain the nightmare in its entirety.

The contents of the dream offer a rare glimpse of human history in a single image. What the king has seen is a great statue made up of four metals (gold, silver, bronze and iron) representing four earthly kingdoms. In the end the statue is struck by a 'rock' that is 'cut out' of a mountain, but *not by human hands* (Dan. 2.45), causing it to be broken into fragments and scattered across the earth.

Here again we see the hallmarks of the same epic spiritual struggle that we have seen rages throughout the Bible, from Genesis to Revelation. On the one hand we see four kingdoms, representing the summit of human achievement, which appear towering and invincible on the outside. On the other hand we see nothing but a rock, recalling the single stone with which David felled Goliath. Yet this is no ordinary stone: the phrase 'not by human hands' suggests that it is not of human origin: elsewhere the image of a divine 'stone' or 'rock' is a picture of God himself (Gen. 49.24; Deut. 32.4; Is. 8.14).

In effect the Bible comes full circle at this point. We are actually seeing the story of Genesis 11 spelt out yet again in fresh imagery. Here Babel, the original pinnacle of human achievement, and the first of the empires portrayed in the statue, is presented as part of an edifice that is tall, imposing and apparently indestructible. Yet, just as the ill-fated builders of the original Babel were vulnerable through their internal divisions, so the statue is also unstable at its weakest point - where there are disunited substances (the iron and clay). The fate of the statue, like Babel, is to be scattered across the earth.

However, Nebuchadnezzar's dream goes beyond the Babel story in two important ways. To begin with, the rock which strikes the statue in Daniel 2 does not simply destroy it. Rather, it expands to a mountain that fills the whole earth, replacing the statue with something infinitely larger and more powerful.

Secondly, it is not a single kingdom that is struck, but a composite of four different empires (represented by the different metals). Until the eighteenth century, both Christian and Jewish commentators have been reasonably consistent in identifying these four kingdoms as Babylon, Persia, Greece and Rome, though other competing interpretations have since been put forward.[1]

In a sense, then, the dream is offering us a glimpse of the entire span of human history. Such snapshots of history were not unknown in later Jewish writings. The same fourfold pattern is also adopted in 2 Baruch 39 and 4 Ezra 11. Likewise, the Sibylline Oracles (at least partly Jewish in origin) present ten empires of world history culminating in a golden age, and a similar scheme appears in the 'Apocalypse of Weeks' from the Book of Enoch.[2]

The mention of just *four* empires in Daniel, however, may be particularly significant. Four is the number of universality in scripture. There are four directions, four corners of the earth, four winds of heaven, four gospels, and so on. The sheet that was lowered from heaven to declare all foods clean in Acts 10.11-16 was lowered from its four corners. Likewise the New Jerusalem descends as a perfect square (indeed, as a cube!)

marking its universal nature as the ultimate habitation for mankind.

In fact, this very same sequence of ages (gold, silver, bronze and iron) was anticipated in *Works and Days* by the Greek writer Hesiod, who lived around 700 BC (though he included an additional 'Heroic' age between these),[3] and a fourfold scheme based on the same metals also appears later in *Metamorphoses* by the Roman poet Ovid (43 BC - 18 AD).[4] Both envisaged an initial 'golden age' where Eden-like conditions prevailed, and a gradual deterioration of human behaviour through the successive ages up to the 'iron age' of their own day.

A similar fourfold scheme comes back later in Daniel as well, corresponding exactly with the successive stages of the statue that Nebuchadnezzar had seen earlier. Chapter 7 describes four beasts (resembling a lion, a bear, leopard, and an unnamed beast that is 'terrifying and frightening') which are destroyed by the coming of 'one like a son of man'. Tellingly, the last of the beasts that Daniel sees, like the legs of Nebuchadnezzar's statue, is partly made up of iron, while the ten horns it possesses clearly match the statue's ten toes.

Revelation, meanwhile, presents us with yet another variation on the same theme. Now we see a *single* beast ruling over the earth who appears to be a composite of all Daniel's four, having the appearance of a leopard, feet like a bear's and a mouth like a lion's, as well as ten horns (13.1-2). As in Daniel 7, the ten horns represent ten rulers who are subservient to the beast (Dan. 7.24; Rev. 17.12-13). Once more the beast is consigned to everlasting destruction through the triumphant return of Jesus (19.20).

The same underlying story, then, seems to be repeated over and over again in different guises throughout scripture. And this in turn raises a question. Could Babylon, Greece and Rome just be representative names for a single, evolving spiritual reality? And if so, could that reality still be present with us today? Saddam's own fate reminds us how history so often returns like a boomerang upon itself.

There are some tell-tale clues in scripture to back this idea up. For instance, 'Babylon' appears to be a code-name for Rome in both 1 Peter 5.13 and Revelation 17.9, where the city is described, like Rome, as sitting on seven hills (by contrast, the original Babylon, set on a completely level plain, had been destroyed many years earlier). And just as Revelation suggests the original glories of the Babylon-to-Rome legacy being revived shortly before Christ's second coming, so the prophecies later in Daniel seem to jump forward imperceptibly from subsequent historical events in Greek and Roman times (the crucified Messiah in 9.26a and the rise of Antiochus Epiphanes in 11.21-32) to 'the time of the end' (9.26b, 11.35,40) when human rebellion is finally defeated and a general resurrection takes place (9.27, 11.45, 12.2).

The same prophetic 'telescoping' applies to Daniel's use of the phrase 'the abomination which causes desolation' (9.27, 11.31). In the apocryphal book of 1 Maccabees (1.54) it is used, as in the second of Daniel's references, to describe the pagan altar that the Seleucid ruler Antiochus Epiphanes built in the temple in Jerusalem. But Jesus applies the same expression to refer to a cataclysmic act of desecration that will take place shortly before he returns (Matt. 24.15).

In the same way, the New Testament jumps forward from 'many tribulations' (Acts 14.22 ESV) to *the* great tribulation (Matt. 24.21 ESV; Rev. 7.14), from 'many false prophets' (Matt. 24.11) to *the* false prophet (Rev. 19.20), from many 'lawless deeds' (2 Pet. 2.8) to *the* lawless one (2 Thess. 2.8-9) and from 'many antichrists' (1 John 2.18) to *the* antichrist (1

John 4.3). It as if history is being wound up like a watch, waiting for its final dénouement.

Stronger evidence that the kingdoms represented in the statue make up a single spiritual reality can be seen in the way that they seem to generate a pattern of opposition towards God's people. Daniel 7.21 talks clearly of a leader springing out of the succession of empires who begins 'waging war against the holy people and defeating them'. Moreover, the four levels of the statue in Daniel 2 and the four beasts of Daniel 7 might perhaps correspond to the 'four horns' that Zechariah sees in a parallel vision, which 'scattered Judah, Israel and Jerusalem', bringing about a terrifying angelic judgement on the perpetrators (Zech. 1.18-21).

Indeed, history furnishes us with a whole catalogue of people throughout history who have sought to outlaw Jewish worship and to annihilate Jews in the process - from Haman and Hadrian in the distant past to Hitler and Hamas in more recent times.

If Jewish tradition preserves any independent record, this pattern of persecution may go right back to the very foundations of Babylon. The Midrash relates that before Abraham's birth, Nimrod, the founder of Babylon, is told that a child would be born who would rebel against his rule. Like Pharaoh and Herod after him, Nimrod's response is to order all new-born babies to be slaughtered. Abraham's mother flees and gives birth to her son in a cave.[5]

Then, when Abraham is older, he refuses to participate in the idolatry around him. Nimrod throws him into a furnace for not bowing down to his gods. However, God delivers him and he escapes unharmed.[6]

Whether there is any truth in these tales or not, the outline appears to follow a template that runs throughout history. We know the same basic storyline reappears later under Babylonian rule (with the fiery furnace) and Persian rule (with the den of lions), along with Haman's attempts under a later Persian king to annihilate the Jews entirely. The same pattern continues later, too, under Greek and then Roman rulers.

We have already mentioned the Greek Seleucid ruler Antiochus Epiphanes, whose name means 'God made manifest'. On December 25th 167 BC he invaded the temple in Jerusalem and established idolatrous worship (the 'abomination that causes desolation' prophesied in Daniel 11.31). He had a pagan altar built on the Great Altar and he put up a statue of Zeus in the Holy of Holies. He made reading or following the Jewish law punishable by death, banned Sabbath-keeping and circumcision, forced the Jews to eat pork, and enforced sacrifices to other gods. House-to-house searches were made each month to make sure that every copy of the Torah was destroyed.

Three years later to the very day Judas Maccabeus, against all the odds, cleansed and rededicated the temple. Hanukkah became the enduring symbol of the victory of the Jews over paganism.

In 63 BC, however, this short-lived period of independence ended when the Roman general Pompey walked into the Most Holy Place of the temple in Jerusalem. Although an uneasy peace prevailed, there were a series of revolts which the Romans often put down by crucifixion.

Tacitus tells us that the Jews' patience ran out when Gessius Florus became procurator in 64-66 AD.[7] According to Josephus, he randomly arrested 3,600 people, including women and children, and had them flogged and crucified (even some who were Roman citizens and should have been exempt from such barbaric treatment).[8] Titus, who oversaw the siege of Jerusalem and the destruction of the temple, also used mass crucifixion to enforce his rule.

After the emperor Hadrian began building a new capital Aelia Capitolina on the ruins of Jerusalem in 131 AD, the Jews revolted again the following year. This time the result was even more drastic - 580,000 Jews were killed, many more were taken into slavery, and all observance of Torah and the Jewish calendar was banned. An altar to Jupiter was erected on what had once been the site of the temple. As a result, many Jews moved back to Babylonia, where they remained until the twentieth century. Only with the founding of the modern state of Israel were they able to return their original homeland.

Meanwhile, under many of the states which succeeded the Roman Empire, the barbaric treatment of Jews continued, with the church often complicit either by its silence or by actual involvement in the persecution. Forced baptisms and conversions, expulsions, Crusades, Inquisition, ghettoes, pogroms, and repeated humiliations mark a sad and harrowing tale that culminates in the unspeakable atrocities of the Holocaust.[9]

One indication that a single spiritual entity might ultimately lie behind these attacks appears in the inexplicable way in which they seem to cluster around one particular date in the Jewish religious calendar, the 9th of Av. Within a day or so on either side of this date a whole series of cataclysmic events in Jewish history took place, marking a horrific cycle of destruction:

- The destruction of the First Temple by the Babylonians in 587 BC
- The destruction of the Second Temple by the Romans in 70 AD

- The ending of the Bar Kokhba revolt against Roman rule in 135 AD
- The expulsion of Jews from England in 1290
- The expulsion of Jews from France in 1306
- The expulsion of Jews from Spain in 1492
- The date Germany entered World War I in 1914, beginning the countdown that led ultimately to the horrors of the Holocaust.
- The authorisation for the 'Final Solution' in 1941
- The first deportation of Jews from the Warsaw Ghetto to the Treblinka concentration camp in 1942

As I pointed out in an earlier book, *The Forgotten Bride*, this alignment of apparently unconnected events can hardly be accidental:

> Before the idea of linking all these events is ruled out of court as yet another wild conspiracy theory, it is worth reminding ourselves that lunar calendar used by the Jews runs out of phase with any other dating system. It is extremely unlikely that any secular power could stage-manage such a series of disasters even if it wanted to. However hard it might be for us to accept with our modern sceptical worldview, it simply beggars belief that so many calamities on this date could be pure coincidence. It bears all the hallmarks of something far more sinister ... the outlines of a co-ordinated spiritual attack.[10]

It does appear, therefore, that there is some kind of veiled spiritual continuity between all the empires represented in the statue and the powers that went on to succeed them. In the next chapter we will consider what implications this has for our understanding of history and the position in which we find ourselves today.

Questions to Consider:

(i) What are the idols that we have allowed to rise up in our own lives? Is there any hold that they may have on us that might deter us from pulling them down?

(ii) Read Daniel chapter 4. What are the similarities in imagery with chapter 2? How was the dream fulfilled in Nebuchadnezzar's personal life? Are there wider principles that can be drawn out? (It might be useful to compare Ezekiel chapter 31).

(iii) Reflect on Isaiah 40.3-8 and 21-31. How do the highs and lows of human history and the sovereignty of great kings and empires appear from God's perspective? What do we learn about our place as believers in the greater scheme of things?

7 A KINGDOM DIVIDED

We noticed in the last chapter that a *single spiritual agenda* seems to be controlling all the empires pictured in the statue and the beasts graphically portrayed in Daniel 7. Outwardly they keep re-inventing themselves, morphing into each other apparently effortlessly. Babylon became the capital of the Persian Empire (the Persian king Cyrus is described as the 'king of Babylon' in Ezra 5.13), and this in turn was absorbed by the Greek Empire under Alexander the Great. Both Cyrus and Alexander attempted to re-establish Babylon as a great centre of learning, and Alexander died in Nebuchadnezzar's palace in 323 BC, planning to establish Babylon as his imperial capital. The Roman Empire subsequently engulfed much of the remains of the Greek Empire, but also continued to expand westwards and northwards.

Like Babel, the Roman Empire was eventually struck at its heart and fragmented. The Latin language which, along with Greek, had held the known world together, diverged into many distinct languages, giving us the Spanish, Portuguese, French, Italian and Romanian tongues of today.

For some Christian commentators throughout history, it might have seemed that Nebuchadnezzar's dream of the rock which struck the statue becoming 'a huge mountain' that 'filled the whole earth' had been fulfilled. The might of the Roman Empire had been supplanted by the power of the Catholic church, which became a 'spiritual' kingdom, worldwide in its extent.

The reality, however, of the final stage of the statue is more complex. Daniel interprets the two feet as representing a divided kingdom (2.41). In 286 AD the emperor Diocletian realised that it was impractical to maintain the Roman Empire as a single, centralised state and experimented with splitting it up. Although Constantine, the first Roman emperor to embrace Christianity, reunited the divided segments, he took the decision to shift the capital of the empire eastwards, effectively creating two competing centres of power and influence. Although his first choice for the 'new Rome' was Troas (just 12 miles from ancient Troy), he discovered that the city of Byzantium, further north, was well fortified and lay not just at the crossroads of several major trade routes, but at the meeting-point of two continents. It also carried the powerful symbolism of being built, like Rome, on seven hills, and accordingly he selected it as his new capital.

At first the newly-ennobled Byzantium (now renamed Constantinople) served as the administrative centre for the whole empire, but after Constantine's death the empire was split between his sons. From 395 AD this separation between western and eastern empires became permanent until the western flank finally collapsed in 476 AD.

The legacy of this division can be seen in the various empires which ended up attempting to succeed the Roman Empire on both western and eastern sides. Long after its original demise,

Pope Leo III gave Charlemagne the title 'Emperor of the Romans' in the west in 800 AD, and through his legacy the Holy Roman Empire endured for centuries: at its height under Charles V, who was crowned Holy Roman Emperor by the Pope in 1530, it included huge swathes of territory in America and Africa. Even after its dissolution, Austrian and later German emperors preserved the title 'Kaiser' ('Caesar') and made of use the Roman imperial eagle on their state insignia.

The impact of the Holy Roman Empire was closely intertwined with the influence of the Vatican, from which papal jurisdiction could be extended over huge areas direct from Rome. Latin, which had been the original language of the western Roman Empire, continued to operate as the language of the Catholic church across the world, centuries after it had ceased to exist as a living language.

In parallel with this, the great powers of the 16th to the 19th centuries who went on to control huge tracts of the world's surface, Portugal, Spain, Britain and France, were all countries originally belonging to the western arm of the Roman Empire, and they imposed the classical architecture of Greece and Rome as symbols of administration and governance wherever they went. Portugal, Spain and France continued to spread the Catholicism of Rome in their wake, while the classical learning central to the British public school system became foundational to the civil service throughout the British Empire.

Out of this wave of military expansionism Napoleon attempted to impose unity across a wide swathe of Europe and the Americas. Modelling himself on the victorious Greek general Alexander the Great, he abolished the Holy Roman Empire which had been in existence continuously for 1,000 years and promulgated his own centralising ideas. "I wished to found a European system, a European Code of Laws, a

European judiciary: there would be but one people in Europe," he was later to write in exile from St. Helena.[1] It was he, not Winston Churchill, who first proposed a 'United States of Europe'. The Napoleonic Code, based on Roman law, underpins legal systems not just across Europe and the Middle East, but as far afield as Quebec, Louisiana and Latin America.

Even as late as the twentieth century, the dream to recreate the glories of the Roman Empire and its successors proved to be a powerful driving-force: we see Hitler attempting to establish a 'Third Reich', while the EU, founded on the Treaty of Rome in 1957, might be seen as a humanistic replacement for the *'pax Romana'*. After a failed attempt by Napoleon, the euro is the first Europe-wide single currency since the Roman imperial system and in the wake of Brexit the union is forging ahead with ever-closer ties. Intriguingly, the European Parliament building in Strasbourg is deliberately modelled on Breughel's famous painting of the Tower of Babel (itself inspired by the Colosseum in Rome).

Meanwhile, in the East another story emerges. The Byzantine church was less and less content to accept the primacy of Rome and in the 11th century the Orthodox church split off from Catholicism. It considered itself the true successor to the apostolic legacy and even today its leading representative is styled 'His Most Divine All-Holiness, the Archbishop of Constantinople, *New Rome*, and Ecumenical Patriarch'.

Constantinople continued to attempt to preserve the legacy of the Roman Empire through the Dark Ages and between the 4th and 12th centuries it remained the largest and wealthiest city in Europe. However, with the rise of Islam the eastern Roman Empire continued to retreat into an increasingly small slice of territory until its final capitulation in 1453, ending almost fifteen centuries of Roman imperial rule since the time of Augustus.

This major rupture caused the centre of gravity in Orthodoxy to shift northwards. Moscow now attempted to set itself up as the *'third Rome'* under Ivan III, who married the niece of the last Byzantine emperor, took the title 'Czar' ('Caesar') and adopted the double-headed eagle of Constantinople as his emblem. Slowly through its new Russian host the Orthodox faith of the eastern Roman Empire began to spread as far as east as the Pacific, across a continent that had otherwise been largely impervious to Christendom.

Yet alongside this another powerful contender for the legacy of Nebuchadnezzar's statue in the East was in the ascent. For centuries Islam had been rising as an alternative outworking of the empires of Babylon, Persia, Greece and Rome. Within a century it had engulfed the whole of Roman north Africa. Baghdad, only 55 miles north of Babylon itself, became by 900 AD the largest city in the world with over one million people, dwarfing the population of every European city for hundreds of years. It controlled a huge Muslim empire with its own single currency and banking system which extended from the Indian to the Atlantic oceans, based on the gold dinar (the successor to the Roman silver *denarius*).

Single-handedly this empire took over and preserved the teachings of leading Greek philosophers such as Plato and Aristotle that had largely become lost in the West. Many early mosques also borrowed the Romanesque design of early Christian churches, with their vaulted spaces, mosaics and columns. Most distinctively their use of domes, closely adapted from Roman and Byzantine models, is still evident across the Islamic world today.

Islam also copied some very negative aspects of the Byzantine imperial system. In particular, much of the legislation governing the inferior *dhimmi* status of Christians and Jews (and the *jizya* tax imposed upon them by their Muslim overlords) seems to have been lifted wholescale from the harsh and discriminatory rules originally imposed upon Jews in the eastern Roman empire. Tragically, Christian minorities in many Muslim countries today are still reaping the bitter fruits of historic misjudgements in the past by supposedly 'Christian' rulers.

Under the weight of its own inefficiency, corruption and complacency, Constantinople, as the last remaining hub of the eastern Roman Empire, fell to the forces of Islam with the invasion of the Turks in 1453, and became the new capital of the Ottoman Empire. Its new ruler, Sultan Mehmet II, who himself had blood descent from the Byzantine Royal Family, adopted the imperial designation 'Kayser-i-Rūm' (Caesar of the Romans) as one of his titles. He promoted the sons of the vanquished last Byzantine emperor to high positions in his court and even had plans to capture Rome itself before his premature death. For at least two hundred years, many educated Ottoman citizens would refer to themselves as 'Rūmī' (Romans) and the Orthodox Church remained the largest holder of land in the empire.

At a strategic juncture between East and West, the Ottoman Empire absorbed much of the legacy of Greece and Rome, but was also heavily indebted in its culture, literature and decorative arts to Persia, the previous segment of Nebuchadnezzar's statue. However, these outside influences were subordinated to the overriding aim of propagating Islam and between 1517 and 1924 Constantinople (later renamed as 'Istanbul') became the seat of the Islamic Caliphate, giving it a worldwide jurisdiction over the Muslim world. Eventually, though, like the mixture of clay and iron in the statue's toes, the same forces of stagnation, corruption, nepotism and complacency that had previously destroyed the Byzantine Empire also brought down the Ottoman Empire in its wake.

There are, as a result, a bewildering number of claimants as standard-bearers of the Babylon/Rome legacy. Given that many of these key players have profoundly shaped the world we now live in, we are faced with an important question. Is the statue still standing spiritually today? Does it continue to determine the course of history?

At first sight there may be little obvious sign of such a controlling influence. All the countries which now correspond to the four original elements in the statue, namely Iraq, Iran, Greece and Italy, appear to be shadows of their former selves. All have undergone, to varying degrees, a measure of profound shaking in recent times.

One possible modification is to see a steady westward travel of the centre of economic power in the world across history. Starting from Babylonia and Persia and moving over to Greece and then Rome, we have seen the torch continuing to pass in more recent times from Britain across the Atlantic to America and then over the Pacific to China, which has for millennia preserved a strong independent civilisation of its own. Having started in what is now the continent of Asia, the torch has finally moved back to Asia once more.

Another possible view is to see the four beasts in the second vision in Daniel 7 as four *new* kingdoms, rising from the ashes of the old, rather than being simply a fresh take on the same kingdoms described in Daniel 2. This interpretation, first proposed in the late 19th century by Sir Robert Anderson, and revived more recently by the late David Pawson, sees the lion that is stripped of its eagle-like wings as Great Britain, shorn of its colonies in the United States, the bear raised up on one side with three ribs in its mouth is Russia, and so on.[2]

A third possibility is for a partial realignment between the legs of the statue from east/west to north/south, with the Mediterranean as a partial buffer in between. The defining conflict at the 'time of the end' in Daniel is, after all, a battle in the Middle East between the 'king of the North' and the 'king of the South' (Dan. 11.40). In today's terms this might suggest a conflict between the West and the increasingly turbulent world of Islam, which operates across both a north/south and west/east axis.

A fourth view diverts some attention away from Rome as a primary link in the chain and focuses the latter part of the succession of empires almost entirely on the rise of Islam. This is the perspective taken up, for instance, in Joel Richardson's book *The Islamic Antichrist*, where he puts forward a very persuasive case for identifying the Beast described in Revelation with the Mahdi, the figure all Shia and many Sunni Muslims expect to appear in the last days to convert the whole earth to Islam. It is perhaps worth noting in this respect that Islamic tradition holds that he will rule from Kufa in Iraq, very close to the historic site of Babylon.

Allowing for all these possible reconfigurations, and the apparent clockwise shift of influence around the world away from the original centres of power, there is every evidence that the spiritual legacy of Nebuchadnezzar's statue still influences us profoundly today. In particular, we see a resurgent Muslim world that increasingly dominates the news agenda and is constantly sparring with the West. The attack on the World Trade Centre and the American invasion of Iraq that followed in its wake represented two of the most significant and iconic events shaping our new century.

We should also not ignore the increase in persecution against Christians on an unprecedented scale, not just in the Muslim world but also in a number of Asian countries outside the Islamic sphere. This recalls the 'little horn' which was to come out of the ten horns that Daniel sees in his vision in chapter 7 (almost certainly corresponding to the ten toes of the statue in chapter 2):

> As I watched, this horn was waging war against the holy people and defeating them, until the Ancient of Days came and pronounced judgment in favour of the holy people of the Most High, and the time came when they possessed the kingdom. (Dan. 7.21-22)

All these factors are symptomatic of an increasingly fundamental clash of values between the East on one side (represented by Russia, China and the Islamic world) and the West on the other. Despite our increasingly globalised world, the two legs of the statue are as far apart as they have ever been. It seems that there is another chapter in this story still to be written, and it may contain many new surprises.

In the midst of all this there is a significant irony. After the 2003 Iraq invasion US forces under the command of General James T. Conway built their military base 'Camp Alpha' on the ancient site of Babylon, levelling parts of the archaeological site to create a landing pad for helicopters and to park heavy vehicles.

History has proved this war to be a strategic disaster, both for the US and for the West generally. It has exacerbated the conflict between the West and militant fundamentalist Islam and given rise to the brutal but thankfully short-lived Islamic State, whose unspeakable atrocities eclipsed even the savagery and cold brutality of Saddam Hussein himself. Even in our own century, therefore, the land of Babylon has exerted a profound influence in world affairs and has led us into a very uncertain future.

Fortunately, as Christians, we are privileged to know the end of the story. Ultimately we know that *every knee will bow* at the feet of Jesus. Each of the dominions represented by the successive stages in the statue ultimately had to recognise this. Nebuchadnezzar, as king of Babylon, finally had to recognise the sovereignty of the God of Israel and even fell prostrate before Daniel (2.46). Cyrus, the Persian emperor, sent out a proclamation throughout the empire acknowledging the rulership of 'the LORD, the God of heaven' (2 Chron. 36.23). Alexander the Great, representing Greece, prostrated himself before the Jewish High Priest in honour of the God he represented (Josephus, *Antiquities of the Jews,* 11.8.5). And Rome itself eventually capitulated to the faith it tried so hard to extinguish.

The gospels also bear witness to this in a small way. The Magi (representing Babylonia and Persia) come to seek out Jesus (Matt. 2.1-2). The Greeks come to seek out Jesus (John 12.20-21). The Roman centurion comes to seek out Jesus (Matt. 8.5-13). The sign on the cross is written in Greek and Latin as well as Aramaic (John 19.20). In the end it is the Roman soldier at the cross who proclaims, 'Surely this man was the Son of God!' (Mark. 15.39).

One day everyone will discover this truth. The world will be taken by surprise. In the heights of complacency, Babylon fell to the Medes in a single night of feasting, just as Isaiah and Jeremiah predicted it would (Is. 13.17-19, 21.1-10; Jer. 51.54-58). In the same way, sudden tribulation will strike the whole earth at a time of 'peace and safety' when all are 'eating and drinking' as in the times of Noah (Luke 17.26-27, 1 Thess. 5.3).

But, as Christians, we need to be ready for this moment. 'When these things begin to take place, stand up and lift up your heads, because your redemption is drawing near.' (Luke 21.28). Now is not a time for complacency. The bridegroom is on his way.

Questions to Consider:

(i) What was it about Rome that caused so many world empires to want to emulate it? In what sense does the Roman dream fulfil the legacy of Babylon?

(ii) Read the accounts in Genesis 16.1-15 and 21.8-21 about Ishmael, who, according to Muslim tradition, is the distant forefather of Muhammad. What light might these passages throw on our understanding of Islam and its current relations with Israel and the West? What beacons of hope are there in these passages for the Muslim world (see also Hebrews 2.16)?

(iii) In what ways can we reach across to different cultures to draw them towards Christ? How might we best express the challenge of the gospel when addressing different backgrounds and worldviews (consider John 3.1-15; 4.4-26; Acts 13.16-41; 17.22-31)?

---

8 THE SHOCK OF THE NEW

The writer of Ecclesiastes comments that 'there is nothing new under the sun' (Ecc. 1.9). Today's fast-paced world poses a severe challenge to this viewpoint. We seem to be embarking headlong on a process of change faster than anything experienced in human history, outside major world revolutions. Old ways of doing things and seeing the world are being discarded and long-established boundary markers are being demolished. Humanity is being driven forward at a dizzying pace into an uncertain and ill-defined future.

One intriguing feature of the statue that we have been considering in the last two chapters is how each level succeeds the previous one. Logic would dictate that it should be built from the earliest stages upwards, like the Tower of Babel itself. However, we find the opposite is the case: it progresses from the top downwards. Effectively, its foundations are upside-down!

There are two results of this. Firstly it shifts from the heaviest and most expensive metals at the top to progressively cheaper metals as we go down. As in the earlier *Life and Works* by the Greek poet Hesiod, everything increases in strength but decreases in value. There is less and less homogeneity and more and more mixture. The materials - gold, silver, brass, iron and clay - become steadily more vulnerable to rust and decay. The statue is struck at its most vulnerable point.

In a sense, the downward trend is a result of the fall. History, scripture and human experience show us how the loftiest ideals are subject to deterioration. The life of Solomon is a case study of losing direction from such strong beginnings. The universe itself is in 'bondage to decay' (Rom. 8.21). The New Testament spells out how these processes work in individuals and humanity as a whole, stage by stage (Rom. 1.21-32; Eph 4.18-19; James 1.14-15).

In society this might involve the gradual breakdown of law and order. In international relations it might represent the slide from stability into tension and all-out conflict. In family life it might result in a gradual erosion of a secure environment in which children can be nurtured. In individuals it might represent a shift from vision-centred, purpose-driven living to passivity, complacency and fatalism.

There are periods when these trends are also mirrored in the arts. Since the Enlightenment we have seen in painting and music what might appear to be a degradation of order from loftier ideals and consensually agreed styles. Atheism, spiritual and sexual experimentation certainly influenced movements from the turn of the twentieth century onwards, leading to an unrestricted free-for-all where anything is acceptable, while remaining largely incomprehensible to a wider public. The famous comment of the influential avant-garde composer Anton Webern (1883-1945) that children would be singing his fragmentary melodies in fifty years' time has proved to be nothing but a mirage.[1]

While the Tower of Babel pictures this progression from man's point of view - 'reach for the skies' - the statue shows things from God's point of view - 'reach for the gutter'. Nebuchadnezzar ends up crawling round on all fours as an animal. That shows the reality of what Babylon is before God, like the beasts in Daniel 7 or Revelation 13.

The second consequence of the 'top down' structure of the statue is that its feet represent the future rather than the past. It is, as a result, rooted at its end, not at its beginning, in an ultimately unknown destiny, rather than in the certainties of what lies beforehand.

Because of this, it has no foundations and can only look forward, never backwards. The Babylonians had no word for 'history'.[2] The result has often been a preoccupation with the new - with progress and with change, with the constant challenging and discarding of old ideas. Respect for elders or for tradition is frequently replaced with a fixation on innovation and on the cult of the young (Alexander the Great died at just 32 years old). Ancestor worship characteristic of traditional cultures gives way to the veneration of youth and modernity. Visions of replacing the failures of the past with utopian visions of the future more often than not beget tragic mistakes such as Nazism and Communism.

And, just as the value of the metals cheapens progressively as we move lower down the statue, the obsession with progress actually gives rise to deterioration. As new things are gained, other more precious things are lost.

In modern times we can see this pattern re-emerge through the Enlightenment, and the exaltation of reason over tradition. The crowning event of the Enlightenment, the French Revolution, provided an opportunity to overthrow corrupt elites and to restart from scratch, following the principles of human common sense. Society was re-ordered. Land reforms were introduced. New decimal systems of measurement were brought in that we still use today and there was even an ill-fated experiment with decimal time.

All these were doubtless well-meaning. There was an attempt to copy and emulate the gospels in compassion and tolerance. The Jews were emancipated and the poor were empowered. Corrupt empires gradually gave way to democratic models.

On paper these were all laudable achievements. But they were all done against a flawed underlying agenda. Without Jesus in the centre, anything we do is doomed to fail from the start.

The Russian Revolution of 1917 reveals this particularly clearly. The attempt to replace the profound social injustices of Tsarist Russia failed on a spectacularly large scale and reduced millions into slavery to a cruel, godless state for seventy years.

As part of this a deliberate assault was made on the nuclear family under the Soviet system. All kinds of relationships were accorded equal legal status with traditional marriage, and abortion and divorce made freely available on demand, a policy only reversed as the toll on society and decreased factory output became increasingly evident in the mid-1930s.

In the West this moral transformation has happened far more gradually. However, the 1960s saw a step change in this pace of movement. 1964 was a particularly significant year in Britain. After thirteen years of unbroken Conservative rule, Harold Wilson's Labour government was swept in with 'the white heat of the technological revolution' which later went on to institute major reforms to the laws on same-sex relationships and abortion. John Robinson's book 'Honest to God', published the previous year and debunking most of the key doctrines of the Christian faith, ushered in a new spiritual climate. In the sphere of music, The Beatles had risen to a status when they were inspiring something approaching worship. Later John Lennon proclaimed that they were 'more popular than Jesus',[3] and for many young people their example led to a pilgrimage into a 'Promised Land' of drug-taking, sexual experimentation and eastern mysticism.

Yet what has all this produced? Out of this great wave of idealistic optimism, all that has emerged are unprecedented levels of depression, mental illness, suicide, family breakdown and drug and alcohol abuse.

Neil Armstrong summed up the spirit of the age when he said, 'One small step for a man; one giant leap for mankind.' For all its symbolic value, his 'giant leap' was actually into a vast, uninhabited wasteland, many thousands of miles from our true home. It might serve as a parable of how we have traded in something infinitely precious for a lonely moral desert, incapable of supporting life.

In a sense, the writer of Ecclesiastes is absolutely right. There *is* nothing new under the sun. Society seems doomed to repeat its mistakes endlessly throughout history because it never seems to learn from them.

If we turn to the opening chapters of Isaiah, describing the state of Israel as a nation seven centuries before the coming of Jesus, for instance, we find ourselves in a world remarkably close to the one we know today. In chapter 1 there is rebellion, ignorance, iniquity and corruption, causing the land to be devoured by foreigners and to be equated with Sodom and Gomorrah (vv. 2-10). Despite an outward show of religion, the city is likened to a prostitute, full of murderers, thieves, bribery and injustice (11-17, 21-23). In chapter 2, we are told of superstition, divination, pagan customs and idolatry (6-8). In chapter 3, the list lengthens: the young are exalted over the old; there is oppression, lack of respect, anarchy and unstable leadership (1-7); there is deception and greed (12-15), and a culture of what might in today's terms be described as a militant LGBT and feminist agenda (9,12,16). Finally, in chapter 5, we see ecological catastrophe, unbridled capitalism, drunkenness, dissipation and corruption (5-12, 18-23).

It seems a small leap up from this to the telling glimpse of the future that appears in Paul's second letter to Timothy:

> There will be terrible times in the last days. People will be lovers of themselves, lovers of money, boastful, proud, abusive, disobedient to their parents, ungrateful, unholy, without love, unforgiving, slanderous, without self-control, brutal, not lovers of the good, treacherous, rash, conceited, lovers of pleasure rather than lovers of God— having a form of godliness but denying its power. (2 Tim. 3.1-5)

Paul's description gives a remarkable insight into the current state of civilisation. And yet we seem to have forgotten his warnings. We continue to plunge headlong into an unknown future with no ethical map to direct us and no moral compass to guide us.

In the last chapter of Daniel the angel predicts that at 'the time of the end … many will rush here and there, and knowledge will increase' (Dan. 12.4 NLT). This pithy statement compresses in a nugget a vast amount of information about the world in which we live today. Not only do we live in a 'global village' where businessmen traverse vast distances on a daily basis, but we see alongside this an exponential growth in knowledge that has the potential to transform everything beyond recognition.

The American designer Buckminster Fuller, who created the 'Knowledge Doubling Curve', noticed that until 1900 the total sum of human knowledge doubled approximately every century. By the end of World War II knowledge was doubling every 25 years. Now in many critical spheres it is doubling once a year on average.

Today we are so caught up in this state of flux that we are scarcely aware of the breakneck speed at which we are travelling. In 1949 the American magazine 'Popular Mechanics' made the then unthinkable prediction that computers in the future might weigh as little as 1.5 tons (at that time they weighed around 30 tons and were up to three storeys high).[4] And yet today a simple greetings card that can play 'Happy Birthday' has more computing power than all the computers in the world from that time put together.[5]

Currently we are on the cusp of dramatic breakthroughs in quantum computing, which have the potential to work trillions of times faster than the world's most powerful supercomputers. Many are going beyond this to explore the concept of 'transhumanism' where the human mind seeks to 'augment' itself with artificial intelligence. The possibilities are virtually limitless, and yet the juggernaut seems to be hurtling forward out of control.

This has led some to talk about a technological 'singularity', a point in time at which technological growth runs irreversibly off-limits, resulting in a takeover of human civilization by forces that can no longer be restrained. In this scenario, artificial intelligence begins improving itself to a degree of superintelligence that far surpasses the sum of all human intelligence.

In his essay 'The Law of Accelerating Returns' in 2001, the distinguished inventor Ray Kurzweil suggests that a technological singularity of this kind might occur around 2045. He begins as follows:

An analysis of the history of technology shows that technological change is exponential, contrary to the common-sense 'intuitive linear' view. So we won't experience 100 years of progress in the 21st century—it will be more like 20,000 years of progress (at today's rate). The 'returns,' such as chip speed and cost-effectiveness, also increase exponentially. There's even exponential growth in the rate of exponential growth. Within a few decades, machine intelligence will surpass human intelligence, leading to The Singularity— technological change so rapid and profound it represents a rupture in the fabric of human history. The implications include the merger of biological and nonbiological intelligence, immortal software-based humans, and ultra-high levels of intelligence that expand outward in the universe at the speed of light.[6]

This prospect becomes all the more chilling when we see unprecedented levels of power for the state to control people's lives. In China it has reached the point where intrusive surveillance of the population is taking place round the clock, monitoring biometric data, movements, conversations, social media contacts and even facial expressions. In some cases CCTV cameras have been installed inside people's homes. This is just surely a few steps back from fully-fledged mind control, where people are reduced to pawns on a chessboard of a merciless state.

The Book of Revelation predicted just such a scenario two thousand years ago. It talks of a 'beast' or antichrist-like figure who forces everyone on the earth to worship it:

> It opened its mouth to blaspheme God, and to slander his name and his dwelling-place and those who live in heaven. It was given power to wage war against God's holy people and to conquer them. And it was given authority over every tribe, people, language and nation. All inhabitants of the earth will worship the beast – all whose names have not been written in the Lamb's book of life, the Lamb who was slain from the creation of the world. (Rev. 13.6-8)

It then goes on to tell of a second 'beast' who rules on behalf of the first, enforces this worship and demands total allegiance:

> It ... forced all people, great and small, rich and poor, free and slave, to receive a mark on their right hands or on their foreheads, so that they could not buy or sell unless they had the mark. (v. 16-17)

Already the technology for such an indelible 'mark' exists today. We are already used to the idea of pets being monitored with implanted microchips. We have become increasingly familiar with a cashless society. The benefits of an implanted human 'chip' which could include all our identity data, bank details and health records could be easily marketed under the guise of convenience, efficiency or national security. So easily, with today's advances in brain implants, where neural pathways can be directed from a distance, this could become a cover for a sophisticated form of mind control where our thoughts are no longer our own.

In fact, moves in this direction are happening all around us. In a preprint article submitted to the bioRχiv website in July 2019, the multibillionaire Elon Musk talks about 'a small implantable device' incorporating 'a single USB-C connector for full-bandwidth data transfer', which is ostensibly for 'the restoration of sensory and motor function and the treatment of neurological disorders'.[7] However, the website of his own Neuralink company states that its long-term vision is 'to create BMIs [brain/machine interfaces] that are sufficiently safe and powerful that *healthy individuals would want to have them*'.[8]

This is not purely science fiction, in other words. Just as quantum computers offer the possibility of reading unimaginable quantities of data, and monitoring every connected device on earth, so one day human minds, augmented by AI, could be linked together within a single matrix of compliance. The Babel dream of 'oneness' might be fulfilled in a way we never thought imaginable, by powers we no longer have the means to overcome.

Although such a dystopian nightmare might represent a worst-case scenario, when we think about the level of deception that Hitler and the Nazis were able to achieve in Germany, an advanced and highly-educated country, simply by using the levers of state propaganda and compelling visual theatrics, buttressed by a heady mix of patriotism, loyalty, and fear of reprisal, we should not become too complacent. Whatever the exact nature of the 'mark of the beast', it represents the ultimate rebellion against God and is answered by one of the most chilling warnings in the entirety of scripture:

> A third angel followed them and said in a loud voice: 'If anyone worships the beast and its image and receives its mark on their forehead or on their hand, they, too, will drink the wine of God's fury, which has been poured full strength into the cup of his wrath. They will be tormented with burning sulphur in the presence of the holy angels and of the Lamb. And the smoke of their torment will rise for ever and ever. There will be no rest day or night for those who worship the beast and its image, or for anyone who receives the mark of its name.' This calls for patient endurance on the part of the people of God who keep his commands and remain faithful to Jesus. (Rev. 14.9-12)

Of course, God is not calling us to live in a state of fear. But we are commanded to remain watchful. Although we may still be a little way off from this critical moment, the quicker we push God out of our society, the faster we invite all these things in. Society has nothing to fear from progress when God is at the centre of things. But if we force God out and enthrone technology in his place, as the West seems more and more inclined to do, the sooner we may find our new 'god' will turn against us and destroy us, with devastating consequences. As Jesus warns us,

> 'Do not give dogs what is sacred; do not throw your pearls to pigs. If you do, they may trample them under their feet, and turn and tear you to pieces. (Matt. 7.6)

In view of this, we need to treat the seductive, glittering world of gadgetry around us with caution. While there is nothing wrong with a pursuit of technology or innovation for the betterment of society, the danger is that it becomes an end in itself, blinding us to the real truth. Karl Marx famously declared that religion is the 'opium of the people'.[9] Now, increasingly, technology takes on that role itself in the endless diet of computer games, virtual reality, musical 'wallpaper', non-stop TV and pervasive social media, which numbs us into submission to the godless agenda around us, and propels us forward like lemmings towards the precipice of complete obliteration.

In these times, when the world around us seems more inclined to call out to Siri or Alexa than to Jesus, we need the gospel more than ever before to transform society. If Wesley and Whitefield were able to rescue Great Britain almost single-handedly in the eighteenth century, the same could happen again in our own day. But we need to feel God's heart for our nation and weep his tears. Nothing short of full-blown revival will shake our nation or our world out of its steady death-march towards destruction.

Questions to Consider:

(i)   How good are we at embracing change in our everyday circumstances? Are there times when God has forced change in our lives, against our expectations or desires? What was the result?

(ii)   Read Romans 8.18-25 and Revelation 21.1-5. To what extent do we see today's society held in 'bondage to decay'? What hope does Paul offer for our world? How does God's description of the 'new' in Revelation differ from the way in which the word is generally used today?

(iii)   What is our attitude to the technology which enriches our lives? Do we take it for granted or do we receive it with thankful hearts? How can we stop it from becoming a god that rules us with an iron fist?

9 THE AXE THAT RAISED ITSELF

On the Monday of Holy Week in 2019 the world watched in horror as the ceiling of Notre Dame Cathedral in Paris, one of the most iconic symbols of Christendom, was engulfed in flames. After just ninety minutes the spire had collapsed and there was a real fear that the entire structure would not survive.

In some ways, it was a picture of the ultimate demise of Christian Europe and the final nail in the coffin of a national church that had already capitulated to the onslaught of secularism more than two centuries beforehand. Significantly, it was the day Christians remember Jesus turning over the tables of the money-changers in the temple, and casting out the merchants (Mark 11.15-17). Spiritually, it might be seen as the completion of unfinished business.

The extraordinary background to the whole story makes this a little clearer. Following the French Revolution of 1789, the Catholic Church was banned in France, church lands were confiscated, and many statues, crosses and other signs of worship were plundered or destroyed. Public worship was made illegal and many priests were brutally murdered.

The climax came on November 10, 1793, with the 'Festival of Reason' which saw many church buildings across France transformed into 'Temples of Reason'. In Notre Dame, where the largest of these ceremonies took place, every Christian symbol was covered over and the inscription 'To Philosophy' was carved above the cathedral's doors. In the nave a miniature mountain was constructed, decorated with busts of philosophers, with a Greek temple dedicated to philosophy at its summit. An altar dedicated to Reason was placed lower down the mountain, in front of which a torch of Truth was located.

At the opening a declaration was made that '*le peuple*' would be the new god of the Republic. Later, along with scantily clad dancers, an actress dressed in red, white, and blue, the colours of the Republic, appeared as the Goddess of Liberty, and the congregation then sang out to her, their hands stretched out in worship, a specially composed hymn:

> Come, holy Liberty, inhabit this temple,
> Become the goddess of the French people.

On the face of it this certainly seems like a shocking desecration, as extreme as Antiochus Epiphanes sacrificing a pig in the temple in Jerusalem. And yet it was a significant harbinger of times to come. Indeed, so effective was the impact of the 'Enlightenment' which triggered the French Revolution that today many of our churches have become little more than 'temples of reason' in their own right, purveying human ideas in the guise of religion.

Many reading this will, of course, be extremely sceptical that a fire in a cathedral roof could be connected to something which happened more than two hundred years earlier. But a more recent event at least raises the possibility of a correlation. On

July 9th 1984 a devastating fire broke out in the roof of York minster less than three days after David Jenkins, famous for his denials of a literal virgin birth or resurrection, had been consecrated in the same building as the new Bishop of Durham. David Pawson comments on this event as follows:

> The lightning that struck York Minster came from a small cloud that circled York Minster for 20 minutes in a blue sky. The cloud wasn't big enough for rain, yet it discharged a lightning bolt (without any thunder) that burnt the cathedral from the top down, just after they had renovated it and installed the latest smoke-detection and fire-fighting equipment. Choir boys marching through the cathedral saw it happen, but they heard nothing because there was no thunder at all. I obtained a map of that cloud from the Meteorological Office, and 16 non-Christian meteorologists said that it had to be from God. It was the most unusual thing they had seen in a long time.[1]

The common factor in both cases, of course, is human reason being exalted at the centre of the church in place of God himself (Is. 44.25; Jer 8.8-9). Rather than being willingly squeezed out of the picture, God tells us that 'I will destroy the wisdom of the wise; the intelligence of the intelligent I will frustrate' (1 Cor. 1.19, quoting Isaiah 29.14). When reason tries to become God, something has to give.

The lure of reason is nothing new. Yet the worship of reason in its own right so easily becomes yet another form of idolatry, indistinguishable at root from the worship of carved objects or impersonal forces. Its background goes back to Babel itself and the system of thought it spawned. We have already seen how the statue in Nebuchadnezzar's dream appears to represent a single spiritual entity which appears to regenerate itself in unbroken succession to this very day.

The connection may not be that easy to see at first. The Babylonian system relied heavily on superstition, sorcery and divination (Is. 47.12-13). The interpretation of omens and astrological signs became an exact science to which huge amounts of research were devoted. Their gods were little more than the embodiments of natural phenomena.

An insight into the degree to which such omens influenced major decisions can be glimpsed in Ezekiel:

> For the king of Babylon will stop at the fork in the road, at the junction of the two roads, to seek an omen: He will cast lots with arrows, he will consult his idols, he will examine the liver. (Ezek. 21.21)

By contrast, the Greek culture which developed subsequently placed a much higher value on philosophy and reason. By and large, this worldview is much closer to that which prevails in our modern society today.

However, if there is a single spiritual thread running through these developments (and Josephus hints that the first Greek philosopher, Thales of Miletus, learnt his art in Babylon),[2] could it simply be that the second worldview is simply a more sophisticated adaptation of the first?

Could it be, for example, that with all our strides forward in knowledge, we actually know *less* than we ever did, because in our headlong rush for knowledge we have consigned all understanding of the demonic and the supernatural to the realm of myth and fantasy? Could it be, in fact, that humanism and atheism, far from being a denial of religion, are actually diverting worship *away* from God onto something far more sinister?

The Bible is very clear here. Samuel tells Saul that rebellion is akin to witchcraft (1 Sam. 15.23), while Paul tells us that earthly wisdom is demonic: 'The god of this age has blinded the minds of unbelievers, so that they *cannot* see the light of the gospel that displays the glory of Christ, who is the image of God' (2 Cor. 4.4).

Atheism is Satan's own idea, dressed in the garb of reason. Ultimately it is worship of self, projected onto society, nature or even the universe. If we ourselves are gods (the temptation he originally placed before Eve) then who needs Yahweh?

Babylon cries out, **I am**, and there is none besides me (Is. 47.8). Nineveh, the capital of Assyria, made the same bold claim (Zeph. 2.15). It is striking, therefore, that many centuries later Descartes uttered the foundational cry of the modern age when he said, 'I think, therefore **I am**.'[3] Jesus said that many deceivers would come in his name, saying '**I am**' (Mark 13.6, literally translated).

Increasingly we have made ourselves the **I am** around which everything revolves. In his highly influential book *The Age of Reason* Thomas Paine said, 'My own mind is my own church.'[4] In the 1880s Nietzsche claimed that 'God is dead'.[5]

It is against this background that the French Revolution and the 'Festivals of Reason' which it birthed may be judged. The pervading intellectual climate of the time was dominated by rationalistic interpretations of a God who had once set the ball rolling in creation but had effectively gone into retirement, a philosophy known as 'Deism'.

Elsewhere Unitarianism, which rejected both the pre-existence and the deity of Christ, was also playing a significant role in intellectual thought, diluting much of the teaching of the New Testament to demote Jesus to little more than a great moral example. One of its most influential exponents was Thomas Jefferson, the third US President and one of the drafters of the American Declaration of Independence. His compilation of the gospels from around 1820 (the so-called 'Jefferson Bible') was one of the most audacious attempts since the 2nd century heretic Marcion to rewrite scripture, stripping it of every supernatural reference, miracle, angelic visitation or any reference to the resurrection.

The extent of the reach of Unitarian thought can be judged from the forecast Jefferson once made that 'the present generation will live to see Unitarianism become the general religion of the United States'.[6] Although his prediction was never fulfilled, Harvard University maintained a continuous succession of Unitarian presidents for 123 years from 1810 onwards, a fact that has had a huge impact on the growth of liberal and humanistic thought across America.

In Britain Unitarianism also exerted a powerful influence and its adherents included writers such as Samuel Taylor Coleridge, the pioneering nurse Florence Nightingale, and eminent scientists such as Joseph Priestley, the discoverer of oxygen, and Charles Darwin, whose mother was a Unitarian and who spent a year of his education at a Unitarian school. (The Unitarian church in Shrewsbury contains a memorial tablet declaring that he was 'a member of and a constant worshipper in this church'). The strategic placing of such prominent voices contributed to a gradual drift away in much of the intellectual elite in Britain from orthodox Christian belief.

Across Europe, however, many influential thinkers went far beyond this and attempted to dispense with any faith in God or other supernatural agent. One significant attempt was made by the founder of modern sociology, Auguste Comte (1798-1857), who established a 'Religion of Humanity' in the middle of the nineteenth century. He had temples of humanity built and established a new calendar with months named after famous figures in history such as Shakespeare and Aristotle. Once likened by Thomas Huxley to 'Catholicism minus Christianity',[7] it possessed its own holy trinity of Humanity, Earth and Destiny. Fourteen years of training were required for its prospective priests, who were required to spread a gospel of altruism and to mediate in political and industrial disputes. The High Priest of Humanity was to live in Paris, which was intended to replace Rome as the centre of religion.

In Britain, meanwhile, the Welsh socialist Robert Owen (1771-1858) established Halls of Science across a number of British cities. Each Sunday services would include sermons on philosophical and ethical questions of the day and hymns extolling such virtues as freedom, temperance and altruism. Owen's ideas influenced others such George Holyoake (1817-1906), the last man to be imprisoned for atheism in this country, who created secular hymn books and humanist rituals for marriages and funerals. And in 1878 Richard Congreve of the London Positivist Society founded a 'Church of Humanity' in London following Comte's model in France.

At the same time, within Unitarianism itself and later in Quakerism, there was a steady erosion of the already fragile residue of Biblical values that remained, and a move to espouse an increasingly universalist outlook. When the American preacher Moncure Conway (1832-1907) became the leader of South Place Unitarian Chapel in London in 1864, he gradually steered it away from any distinctively Christian doctrines. Instead, he would incorporate readings from different religions, secular authors, as well as scientific presentations.

Today, another movement has taken on this mantle. In early 2013, an atheist church called 'Sunday Assembly' was launched by two stand-up comedians in a deconsecrated church in

Islington, London, which has now sprouted congregations in more than 40 cities around the world. A report in the BBC News Magazine by Brian Wheeler on February 4th 2013 described an early service, with the theme of 'wonder'. During the service the congregation sang Queen's *Don't Stop Me Now*, Stevie Wonder's *Superstition* and Nina Simone's '*Ain't Got No*' and bowed their heads for two minutes in contemplation about the miracle of life. Also included was a reading from Alice in Wonderland and a power-point presentation from particle physicist Harry Cliff, explaining the origins of antimatter theory.[8]

Adopting Conway's legacy in a deliberate way, Sunday Assembly now meets in Conway Hall, the place to which the South Place congregation transferred in the 1920s.

This need to gather together even in the absence of religious belief is striking. As human beings we are by nature worshippers. 'Atheism' is often a blank cheque enabling people to confer deity on some other object, whether it be humanity, nature, reason or science. Yet it can never replace the fact that God has put 'eternity in the human heart' (Ecc. 3.11). When worship is misdirected, it only produces heartbreak in the long run.

One of the deadliest forms of atheism is the religion of the state and the idolatry of leaders. Lenin commented that 'every religious idea, every idea of God, even flirting with the idea of God, is unutterable vileness ... of the most dangerous kind, "contagion" of the most abominable kind. Millions of sins, filthy deeds, acts of violence and physical contagions ... are far less dangerous than the subtle, spiritual idea of God decked out in the smartest "ideological" costumes ...'. [9]

What he replaced it with, for many people who chose to stand against him, was grim in the extreme. When we create a spiritual vacuum, something has to fill it (Matt. 12.43-45). We only need to look at North Korea today to see the results.

While we may have escaped this in the West we have simply embraced polytheism instead. We have gods of commerce, in whose brightly-lit and marble-paved shrines we sacrifice our hard-earned money to gain retail atonement. We have temples to the gods of music and sex in our nightclubs with their hypnotic, mesmeric beat in which DJs act as the priests of the new religion of youth and hedonism. We have offerings to the gods of luck and fate - the stock exchange being set aside for the rich and the lottery for the poor. We have gods of health, well-being and happiness whose priests are doctors, psychologists, nutritionists and therapists dispensing miracles in hospitals and clinics. And of course we have the constant cult of celebrity whose lives are as colourful as the gods and goddesses of Greek and Roman culture.

And yet for all this we are empty inside, devoid of meaning and purpose. We have no fundamental identity because we have no cosmic past and apparently no eternal destiny. What passes as 'atheism', but is in reality often a confused polytheism, has no value to offer the individual and no ultimate sense of right and wrong to guide humanity.

For centuries mankind has wrestled with the issue of how sinful mankind can stand in the presence of a holy God and give account. Atheism and its various modern equivalents solve the whole problem by airbrushing it out of existence, letting us all off the hook. The Russian philosopher Mikhail Bakunin, a central inspiration behind modern Anarchism, took the famous maxim of the Deist Voltaire that 'if God did not exist, it would be necessary to invent him' by stating that 'if God really existed, it would be necessary to abolish him.'[10]

Implicitly, then, atheism is a denial of the reality that we see around us. The fact that in one survey nearly 70% of self-avowed 'atheists' were actually found to be men suggests that the philosophy has more to do with a projection of male ego than being a genuine answer to the fundamental questions of existence.[11] The end-result is simply to beckon us into a *cul-de-sac* of utter meaninglessness.

Agnosticism, meanwhile, is simply a softer version of the same delusion, committing the same crime through neglect. The only appearance of the word *agnostos* in the New Testament is at Acts 17.23, where it describes the altar in Athens 'to an unknown god', which, as Paul explains, is simply the real God who has been there all the time, but appears to have been completely overlooked. And its modern sibling, *philosophia*, also only appears once, in Colossians 2.8, where it is paired with words meaning 'hollow' and 'deceptive'. J.B. Phillips' colourful translation runs as follows:

> Be careful that nobody spoils your faith through intellectualism or high-sounding nonsense. Such stuff is at best founded on men's ideas of the nature of the world and disregards Christ!

Society has been robbed by a lie that is slowly destroying it from within. The universe declares the glory of God (Ps. 19.1) and yet we have made ourselves blind. As the Psalmist reminds us, 'The fool says in his heart, "There is no God" ' (Ps. 14.1; 53.1). For so many today everything is simply an accident, an illusion or an impersonal machine. The Old Testament repeatedly points out the futility of such ideas:

Does the axe *raise itself* above the person who swings it, or the
saw boast against the one who uses it? As if a rod were to
wield the person who lifts it up, or a club brandish the one
who is not wood! (Is. 10.15)

You turn things upside down,
   as if the potter were thought to be like the clay!
Shall what is formed say to the one who formed it,
   "You did not make me"?
Can the pot say to the potter,
   "You know nothing"? (Is. 29.16)

Do any of the worthless idols of the nations bring rain?
   Do the skies themselves send down showers? (Jer. 14.22)

It is also worth including here the colourful, if rather loose,
paraphrase of Proverbs 30.1-6 by Eugene Peterson in *The
Message*:

The skeptic swore, "There is no God!
   No God!—I can do anything I want!
I'm more animal than human;
   so-called human intelligence escapes me.

"I flunked 'wisdom.'
   I see no evidence of a holy God.
Has anyone ever seen Anyone
   climb into Heaven and take charge?
   grab the winds and control them?
   gather the rains in his bucket?
   stake out the ends of the earth?
Just tell me his name, tell me the names of his sons.
   Come on now—tell me!"

The believer replied, "Every promise of God proves true;
   he protects everyone who runs to him for help.
So don't second-guess him;
   he might take you to task and show up your lies."

It does, of course, all depend on one's final frame of reference.
We will therefore leave the last word to one of the most

outspoken modern proponents of atheism, Christopher Hitchens, who once declared the following:

> "Owners of dogs will have noticed that, if you provide them with food and water and shelter and affection, they will think you are god. Whereas owners of cats are compelled to realize that, if you provide them with food and water and shelter and affection, they draw the conclusion that *they* are gods."[12]

There is one question that faces us, therefore: given all the blessings that have been indiscriminately showered upon the human race, does it make sense to follow the dogs or the cats?

Questions to Consider:

(i) To what extent does the pervasive hold of 'reason' in our society extinguish our consciousness of the supernatural? How might this impede our prayer life and our expectation of the miraculous, and how can we counter this?

(ii) Read Luke 11.24-26. What was the consequence of leaving the house empty? What are the risks to our nation and in our own lives of well-meaning but godless reform, leaving a vacuum at the centre?

(iii) The atheist Christopher Hitchens once described heaven as 'a place of endless praise and adoration, limitless abnegation and abjection of self; a celestial North Korea'. What assumptions are mistaken here, and how might we answer them?

---

10 THE GENDER AGENDA

The climax of the conflict between 'Babylon' and God's kingdom in the gospels comes when Jesus is brought before Pilate in John chapter 18. It is a dramatic moment when two previously distinct sources of authority suddenly appear face to face, the highest secular power in the land versus the king of the universe himself.

The key element in the exchange hinges on the nature of 'truth'. Jesus talks about 'truth' as an absolute quality: he *is* that truth. Pilate, on the other hand, experienced politician though he is, seems to find himself out of his depth. He famously responds in a dismissive putdown: 'What is truth?' (v. 38).

On the one hand, Pilate's question seems strangely up-to-date. He could have been living in the twenty-first century. For us today, as for him, there is no truth, but simply an unbroken continuum of possibilities which are all equally valid.

Yet on the other hand, there is nothing fundamentally new about Pilate's response at all. It is an inevitable outworking of the serpent's original question, 'Did God really say …?'

Truth is either a closed system or an open system. Once we have removed one moral absolute, we have effectively removed them all. In the short term we end up with moral anarchy ('everyone does what is right in their own eyes') and in the long term with complete moral inversion:

> Woe to those who call evil good
>   and good evil,
> who put darkness for light
>   and light for darkness,
> who put bitter for sweet
>   and sweet for bitter. (Is. 5.20)

Much of today's world is in moral freefall. We demand self-expression, and yet we lose all sense of identity in the process. We crave happiness, and yet we have surrendered every boundary that makes such happiness meaningful. We have tried to buy ourselves freedom, and have ended up with slavery in another disguise.

There is only one possible anchor that could provide meaning and secure us from sliding off the moral precipice, and this has been the custodian of our national identity for centuries. Yet that anchor, the Bible, is ruled out of court *precisely because* it clings to what seem to be archaic absolutes from another age. Too often, it is seen as part of the problem, rather than as being the solution.

For Christians this is a real challenge. We have a message of life that is unique and revolutionary. But are we to paper over the message of scripture to make it more palatable to the outside world or are we going to let our 'yes' be 'yes' and our 'no' be 'no'?

The difficulty is that the Bible is a book of binary opposites. It does not sit comfortably within a post-modernist spectrum.

Instead, it lines light up against darkness, truth against falsehood, and life against death in very stark terms.

It is all too easy to forget that the universe itself is founded on these polarities: positive versus negative, matter versus anti-matter, one versus zero. Without harnessing such principles we would have no electricity, no computers, or anything that enables the modern world to work.

And this clear process of separation, division, contrast and antithesis is evident from the very first page of the Bible. God *speaks* and separates the light from the darkness. He separates the earth from the sky and the land from the sea.

Furthermore, the final and crowning act of this process of separation in Genesis 1 is when God creates a fundamental distinction within humanity that reflects his own innermost being:

> Then God said, 'Let *us* make mankind in *our* image, in our likeness, so that they may rule over the fish in the sea and the birds in the sky, over the livestock and all the wild animals, and over all the creatures that move along the ground.'

> So God created mankind in his own image,
>   in the image of God he created them;
>   **male and female he created them**. (Gen. 1.26-27)

The distinction between genders is a fundamental 'given' of creation. It is a projection of God's own personality and the very 'glue' through which all the other parts stick together. We can read this clearly in the commission which follows:

> God blessed them and said to them, 'Be fruitful and increase in number; fill the earth and subdue it. Rule over the fish in the sea and the birds in the sky and over every living creature that moves on the ground.' (1.28)

Here we see clearly that God has tied our dominion over the natural world to multiplication and fruitfulness. Take away the multiplication and the binary distinction between the sexes that underlies this and you take away the dominion.

Jesus warns us clearly of the danger of tampering with this divine ordinance:

> 'Haven't you read,' he replied, 'that at the beginning the Creator "made them male and female," and said, "For this reason a man will leave his father and mother and be united to his wife, and the two will become one flesh"? So they are no longer two, but one flesh. *Therefore what God has joined together, let no one separate.*' (Matt. 19.4-6)

The second chapter of Genesis throws more light on this. Because God removes something from Adam in order to create Eve, he is incomplete without her. Something is missing that can only be restored in togetherness.

In other words, man is fundamentally incomplete without woman and woman without man. Alec Motyer talks of 'the male and female components of a single reality'.[1] Paul expresses it like this:

> Nevertheless, in the Lord woman is not independent of man, nor is man independent of woman. For as woman came from man, so also man is born of woman. But everything comes from God. (1 Cor. 11.11-12)

John Stott writes as follows:

> 'Heterosexual intercourse in marriage is more than a union; it is a kind of reunion. It is not a union of alien persons who do not belong to one another and cannot appropriately become one flesh. On the contrary, *it is the union of two persons who originally were one, were then separated from each other, and now in the sexual encounter of marriage come together again.*'[2]

In his letter to the Ephesians, Paul links this picture of mutual wholeness of marriage to the relationship between Christ and the church (5.22-23), which is 'the fullness of him who fills everything in every way (1.23). The marriage bed is a picture of the temple itself where God dwells in all his glory (1 Cor. 6.15-20).

Given the challenge that this poses to the kingdom of darkness, it is small wonder that the institution of marriage has been under such sustained attack in recent times. For over three centuries between 1539 and 1857, for example, just 317 marriages in Britain ended in full-scale divorce.[3] For most of the last fifty years, however, this rate was easily exceeded *every single day*.[4] Over forty per cent of marriages now end this way.

More fundamentally, however, the very essence of marriage has now been redefined beyond recognition, not just in Britain, but across the Western world. The Biblical view of marriage as being exclusively between a man and a woman no longer holds sway. We have moved the benchmarks in a manner unthinkable even a generation ago.

Jesus warned of something called the 'abomination of desolation' in the end times, quoting from the prophet Daniel (Mark 13.14). He defined this as something occupying the holy place of the temple that should not be there. Paul defines our bodies as temples of the Holy Spirit. He likens sexual impurity to a defiling of that temple (1 Cor. 6.18-20).

In the Bible the word 'abomination' is not used lightly: it is used both to single out same-sex liaisons in Leviticus 18.22 and 20.13, and as a description for the immorality of end-time Babylon in Revelation 17.5.[5] It is striking, therefore, that the instruction that the angels give to Lot to 'flee to the mountains' in order to rescue him from the impending divine judgement on Sodom (Gen. 19.17), is identical to the one Jesus gives about the 'abomination of desolation' in Mark 13.14.

Might there be a link between these two things? Could we be facing God's judgement on our chaotic attempts to redefine marriage and gender? Are we even now reaping the 'wrath of God' that Paul warns about in Romans 1.18?

It is certainly worth noticing that Satan has tried to destroy marriage from its very inception. Firstly he tried to destroy the glue of sexual relationships by turning Adam and Eve against each other (Gen. 3.12-13). Then he tried to redefine the boundaries of sexual activity by encouraging unauthorised liaisons between human and angelic beings (Gen. 6.1-4). Finally he turned the fragile parity of gender on its head by unleashing a sexual free-for-all, including same-sex encounters (Gen. 19.4-9).

What is striking is the level of anger that we see stirred in the heart of God on each of these occasions. In the first instance he throws Adam and Eve out of the Garden of Eden. On the second occasion he sends the flood. In the third example he causes the complete destruction of two cities. Three times in the New Testament the latter two judgements are linked together (Luke 17.26-29; 2 Pet. 2.4-8; Jude 6-7), suggesting a profound connection between them.

The location of the cities of Sodom and Gomorrah is intriguing. The Biblical site lies beside the Dead Sea, at the lowest point that it is possible descend on the earth's land surface. The Dead Sea is so named because, given its depth, it has no possible outlet. Completely landlocked, and consequently clogged with salt and minerals, it cannot support life. Though copiously supplied by the Jordan, it cannot give, but only receive.

In some ways this serves as a picture of the world of same-sex relationships. Certainly, they can often be passionate, deeply-felt and all-consuming. They may seem to be fed by the noblest desires to care and nurture. They can appear to aspire to the loftiest ideals of compassion, respect and devotion. In the end, however, they are incapable of creating life. And however well-disposed towards this alternative lifestyle we might feel in our own minds, the simple biological fact remains that without heterosexual relationships none of us would exist at all.

Of course, from the world's point of view, such an analysis is not just profoundly offensive, but tantamount to committing a 'hate crime', a modern form of blasphemy. Today's hate laws have become the equivalent of yesterday's heresy laws. Anyone questioning them risks dismissal from employment, exile from academia and silencing by social media.

Instead we have a new secular gospel of inclusion and 'tolerance' which embraces anything apart from the views of those who disagree. Just as it stands to reason for most people that all roads lead to God, so all forms of sexual expression are now increasingly seen as being equally valid. For most people today, certainly in the West, traditional marriage and gay marriage are completely equivalent choices.

Part of the problem is with our overall frame of reference. The way we look at sex reflects something of the way we see the cosmos around us. Because God draws us towards himself, sexual expression is a reflection of our higher call, connecting with 'the other'. By contrast, in a universe that is turned inwards on itself, existing for its own sake rather than having an ultimate purpose, it is natural that sexual behaviour also turns in on itself and becomes introspective rather than outward in manifestation, pursuing its own reflection rather than uniting with an opposite to beget new life.

In the final analysis, the issue boils down to how we form judgements of right and wrong. The two trees in the Garden of Eden may have appeared outwardly identical, but the decisive difference was God's clear warning not to eat from the one. We ignore his commands at our peril. We can choose whether to follow the Kingdom principle or the Babylon principle. But whatever our decision, we have to reap the consequences.

Babylon has its own innate logic. In a previous chapter we pointed out how Nebuchadnezzar's statue, which displays the Babylon principle most clearly, implies an exact inversion of all divine values, by progressing from top to bottom, rather than bottom to top. By nature sexual values might be included in this inversion. It is an 'undivine exchange' which substitutes 'sweet for bitter, bitter for sweet, light for darkness, and darkness for light', as we saw earlier in Isaiah 5.20. According to Ezekiel 16.49-50, the sin of Sodom originated in pride, ease and excess, attitudes which are key characteristics of the Babylonian worldview.

Babylon, like Egypt, was a polytheistic society, but whereas the Egyptians were very concerned with the afterlife, Babylon seems largely concerned with 'now'. Happiness and prosperity in this life were much more important than the concerns about what lay beyond. The gods followed the same unscrupulous behaviour and flawed characteristics as humans and therefore set no overarching moral example. As we noted in the last chapter, sorcery, divination and astrology were used extensively to predict and control events. God twice links the impending destruction of Babylon to that of Sodom and Gomorrah (Is. 13.19, Jer. 50.40).

By and large, the same hedonism was true in Greek and Roman societies. 'Let us eat and drink for tomorrow we die' might have been an appropriate adage (Is. 22.13; 1 Cor.15.32). Many Greek philosophers such as Aristippus and Epicurus held that the pursuit of pleasure and comfort was the highest human good. There was little conception of future judgement and Judaism and Christianity were a unique challenge in this respect. Traditional morality was often something laughed at. Homosexual relationships played a central role in the intellectual man-centred civilisation of both Greece and Rome.

The same is even more true today. Our society lives for the moment but despises tomorrow. We talk about 'disposable income' and fritter away vast quantities of money on unnecessary items. We toss away huge amounts of food each day as refuse while half the world starves. We progressively disfigure our landscapes with a steady accumulation of disposable cans, disposable plastic, disposable nappies and a panoply of other items, and think nothing of it. Most shamefully of all, we are inexorably turning our world into a graveyard of disposable lives, with the merciless slaughter of our unborn in vast numbers at the altar of the god of convenience.

It is little surprise, therefore, that for much of today's world sex has become a throwaway act with no lasting value, or at best the sealing of a temporary contract which can be broken at any time by either party. It is devalued to the point of becoming worthless. This is a total antithesis to the role of sex in the Bible, in which it is an utterly sacred act that begets infinity.

In all this, there are hidden forces acting behind the scenes. Just as there is a spiritual reality underlying the statue in Nebuchadnezzar's dream, so there is a hidden supernatural reality animating and spearheading the LGBT agenda, for all its superficial idealism and apparently benign intentions. A huge reversal of opinion in an incredibly short space of time, pushed by the media, suggests that pieces are being moved around on the spiritual chessboard to an unprecedented degree.

As far back as 1970, Shulamith Firestone, in her book *The Dialectic of Sex* argued that

> [The] end goal of feminist revolution must be, unlike that of the first feminist movement, not just the elimination of male privilege **but of the sex distinction itself** ... The reproduction of the species by one sex for the benefit of both would be replaced by (at least the option of) artificial reproduction: children would born to both sexes equally, or independently of either ... the dependence of the child on the mother (and vice versa) would give way to a greatly shortened dependence on a small group of others.[6]

Fundamentally this manifests not just in an attack on everything we know about humanity but an attack on God himself. Denying the whole order of creation denies the very creator who put it all into place. Proverbs warns about the effect of removing ancient boundary stones (22.28; 23.10). When 'everyone does what is right in his own eyes' moral anarchy ensues and *we* take the place of God.

Isaiah 24 seems to warn of the devastating worldwide consequences that result from tampering with the divine order of creation, established in the universal covenant with mankind which God originally made in Genesis 1.26-29 and 9.7-27:

> The earth dries up and withers,
>   the world languishes and withers,
>   the heavens languish with the earth.
> The earth is defiled by its people;
>   *they have disobeyed the laws,*
> *violated the statutes*
>   *and broken the everlasting covenant.*

> Therefore a curse consumes the earth;
> its people must bear their guilt. (Is. 24. 4-6)

Today we are inclined to see climate change as a purely environmental problem triggered by over-consumption. While the Bible is emphatic that we have a direct responsibility to tend and safeguard the earth (Gen. 2.15, Rev. 11.18), it is clear from the passage we have just read (and many other similar ones) that our moral actions in redefining God-given absolutes trigger unforeseen spiritual consequences that have the potential to impact the environment around us in catastrophic ways.

What, then, has brought us to this point? Perhaps the most profound insight in scripture into the roots of sexual confusion and the realignment of gender appears in chapter 1 of Paul's letter to the Romans. This is a passage that speaks volumes into the society in which we find ourselves today:

> For although they knew God, they neither glorified him as God nor gave thanks to him, but their thinking became futile and their foolish hearts were darkened. Although they claimed to be wise, they became fools and exchanged the glory of the immortal God for images made to look like a mortal human being and birds and animals and reptiles.

> Therefore God gave them over in the sinful desires of their hearts to sexual impurity for the degrading of their bodies with one another. They exchanged the truth about God for a lie, and worshipped and served created things rather than the Creator – who is for ever praised. Amen.

> Because of this, God gave them over to shameful lusts. Even their women exchanged natural sexual relations for unnatural ones. In the same way the men also abandoned natural relations with women and were inflamed with lust for one another. Men committed shameful acts with other men, and received in themselves the due penalty for their error.
>
> (Rom. 1.21-27)

It is important to notice the sequence here, as it is very relevant to the centuries leading up to our own. The first step of mankind's headlong descent to the abyss was to *serve* created things as substitutes for God. During the 18th and 19th centuries theologians began substituting their *own* ideas about God for what the Bible says. *Professing themselves* to be wise, they became fools, by turning against fixed certainties and *setting themselves up* in the place of God as arbiters between truth and falsehood, right and wrong (v. 22).

Secondly, we need to bring the impact of Darwin into the mix. The Greek philosopher Anaximander had over two thousand years earlier proposed the idea that man and all other animals were ultimately descended from fish. Reviving these ideas, the net result of Darwin's philosophy was to substitute Adam as 'son of ape' for 'son of God'. Man, as the 'glory of the immortal God' became demoted to become an offshoot of 'birds and animals and reptiles' (v. 23).[7] Regardless of one's opinions about evolution or the age of the earth, the entire symmetry and integrity of scripture underlines the fact that the creation of Adam is as unique and unparalleled an event as the incarnation of Christ (Rom. 5.15-19; 1 Cor 15.22).[8]

Thirdly, we can see a seismic overturning of the established order in the wider realm of thought at the turn of the twentieth century. As we noted in Chapter Eight, there was an extraordinary revolution in the arts at this time where traditional values were turned upside-down and carefully worked-out rules thrown out of the window. Freud and psychoanalysis charted a new voyage of discovery into the unconscious. There was a significant turning from God to the occult and spiritual experimentation. They 'exchanged the truth about God for a lie, and worshipped and served created things' (v. 25).

While these were all by and large impacting the intellectual and artistic elites of society, it was only a matter of time before their effects would be felt in society at large. As we have already pointed out, it was not until the 1960s that this moral tsunami struck land with full force. Further boundaries began to be eroded and nothing was deemed any longer to be impossible.

Today we are still reaping the consequences exponentially. We have 'sown the wind and reaped the whirlwind' (Hos. 8.7). One reversal of the natural order leads to another. Create a vacuum and something else fills it. Swapping God for something else produces other kinds of substitutions (including sexual substitutions). Paul warns how when we turn our backs on God he 'gives us over' to both sexual and moral degradation, with a deadening of conscience that results (v. 26-27).

Instead of the fundamental pairings of the early chapters of Genesis - light and darkness, truth and falsehood, right and wrong, and now increasingly male and female - everything is placed on a morally neutral spectrum, in which the rainbow, the symbol of God's divine grace, is misappropriated to be a logo for universal licence. Within the span of just a few generations we have gone from clear black and white to fifty shades of grey. Facebook now offers almost sixty different gender options for new users to choose from.

Alongside this is the hijacking of language in order to advance particular ideological goals. Not only do we see an increasing privatisation of pronouns ('they' becoming a popular alternative to 'he' or 'she'), but a whole battery of new words such as 'cisgender' (to devalue those who accept their God-given gender identity); 'otherkin' (adopted by those who self-identify as other-than-human) or the extraordinary 'chestmilk' (instead of 'breastmilk') and 'birthing parent' (instead of 'mother') being pioneered by Brighton and Hove University

Hospitals Trust, who now run 'perinatal' instead of 'maternity' services.[9]

More disturbing is the increasing tendency of the profoundly illiberal 'liberal' establishment to shut down legitimate debate on these issues. The Scottish Parliament in 2021 passed a 'Hate Crime' bill which restricts even what people can say in the privacy of their own homes. At Westminster, meanwhile, attempts to stamp out so-called 'gay conversion' therapy have the potential to criminalise even certain kinds of prayer, despite a clear Biblical mandate for such ministry to take place (1 Cor. 6.9-11). This leads to the ludicrous situation that, while a wide open door has been left for individuals to change their *sex*, someone seeking help to change their *sexuality* could be implicating someone else in a criminal act. The church may yet have to choose whether to wilfully disobey the government and remain true to scripture, or become, like the Chinese 'official' church, an obedient poodle of the state.

So what message should the church be giving out at this time? First and foremost, it is our urgent duty to proclaim clearly the unambiguous message of scripture. As Paul writes,

> in the case of lifeless things that make sounds, such as the pipe or harp, how will anyone know what tune is being played unless there is a distinction in the notes? Again, if the trumpet does not sound a clear call, who will get ready for battle?
>
> (1 Cor. 14.7-8)

However, in doing so, we should remember the danger of using labels and generalisations. We are all sinners. However firmly we nail our colours to the mast of the Bible, we should not be laying down heavy weights on human beings who are utterly precious in God's sight. By a clumsy and heavy-handed response in the past the church has driven people away, and dispensed shame and condemnation, with great injustice to the complex psychological and emotional issues involved.

In particular, 'let him who is without sin cast the first stone'. None of us have earned the right to point the finger. We have all fallen. The institutional church, with its highly chequered record, is in an incredibly weak position to make moral pronouncements. Our deepest instinct should be to show love, care and compassion to those around us, and to focus first and foremost on putting our own hearts and intentions right before God. There is only a difference of one letter between 'immorality' and 'immortality', and that letter is in the shape of the cross, where all sin, great and small, stands on a level playing-field before God.

At the same time, we should not ignore the wider spiritual dimension. We need to recognise that there are not just natural forces at work here, but supernatural powers of deception and mind control, and that they operate universally across the globe. This is hinted at on several occasions in scripture. Jeremiah 51.7 tells of how Babylon 'made the whole earth **drunk**':

> The nations drank her wine;
> therefore they have now **gone mad**.

Similarly, in Revelation, Babylon is told that 'by your **magic spell** all the nations were led astray' (18.23), because 'the inhabitants of the earth were **intoxicated** with the wine of her adulteries' (17.2).'

Likewise, Hosea talks of a '**spirit of prostitution**' which actively immobilises its victims and prevents them from returning to God (Hos. 5.4; see also Proverbs 5.22).

Paul provides more insight into these forces in his letter to the Thessalonians:

For the **secret power of lawlessness** is already at work; but the one who now holds it back will continue to do so till he is taken out of the way. And then the lawless one will be revealed, whom the Lord Jesus will overthrow with the breath of his mouth and destroy by the splendour of his coming.

The coming of the lawless one will be in accordance with how Satan works. He will use all sorts of displays of power through signs and wonders that serve the lie, and all the ways that wickedness deceives those who are perishing. They perish because they refused to love the truth and so be saved. For this reason God sends them **a powerful delusion** so that they will **believe the lie** and so that all will be condemned who have not believed the truth but have delighted in wickedness.

(2 Thess. 2.7-12)

With this in mind we should remember his encouragement to the Ephesian church that our battleground is marked by prayer, not by engaging in controversy or 'holier-than-thou' judgements, and that the battle is directed not against the visible world around us, but rather the invisible forces that lie behind it:

For our struggle is **not against flesh and blood**, but against the rulers, against the authorities, against the powers of this dark world and against the spiritual forces of evil in the heavenly realms. Therefore put on the full armour of God, so that when the day of evil comes, you may be able to stand your ground, and after you have done everything, to stand. (Eph. 6.12-13)

In all these things, therefore, it is essential to keep a careful balance. Jesus warns us to be 'as shrewd as snakes and as innocent as doves' (Matt. 10.16). He came 'full of grace and truth' (John 1.14). In the past grace has been in very short supply within the church on the issues of gender and sexuality, but some in the church today are running away from truth in reaction. Let us therefore pray for God's vision and insight on this complex but critical issue that is central to the times in which we exist, and to live out his Kingdom to the full, seeking purity and holiness in our own hearts but graciousness, respect and compassion in all our dealings with others.

Questions to Consider:

(i)   How might we answer Pilate's question, 'What is truth?' What are the consequences of truth in relative, rather than absolute, terms? In what areas of our lives might we have unconsciously succumbed to this type of thinking?

(ii)   Read the story of Lot in Genesis 13.5-13 and 19.1-26. What was it that first drew him to Sodom, and why was he reluctant to leave?

(iii)   How can we keep our hearts pure before God? Why is it important to examine our thoughts and motives under the microscope, but at the same time to be gentle and considerate towards others (Matt.7.1-5)? What can we learn from the example of Jesus in displaying grace and truth in full measure (John 8.3-11)?

---

11 THE MIRACLE OF COMMON GRACE

From what we have considered so far, we might easily conclude that Babylon and its legacy stands diametrically opposed to everything God has planned for our world. It would be easy to assume that nothing good or worthwhile could emerge from such a proud and godless culture. In Revelation Babylon is described as 'THE MOTHER OF PROSTITUTES AND OF THE ABOMINATIONS OF THE EARTH' (17.5).

We are all doubtless familiar with the proverb, 'the road to hell is paved with good intentions' (based on Sirach 21.10 which is in the Apocrypha). Even Satan was initially perfect until a small trace of evil was found in him (Ezek. 28.15). A dead fly ruins a whole bottle of ointment (Ecc. 10.1). The fallen nature of Nebuchadnezzar's statue determines that everything gradually becomes corrupted, no matter how outwardly impressive it is.

However, it is worth taking a step back before being too hasty in our judgements. The reverse side of the coin is that the Bible throws a positive light on many aspects of human civilisation. We hear, for example, of Nebuzaradan, the enlightened Babylonian official who extended kindness to Jeremiah after the direct personal intervention of Nebuchadnezzar himself (Jer. 39.11-14). We also discover the benign influence of some sympathetic Greek and Roman authorities in the New Testament (Acts 23.12-30; 28.7), and the calming impact of Greek civilisation against an unruly mob (Acts 19.23-41).

In fact, the surprising thing about Babylon and so many great civilisations was not that so much was wrong, but rather that so much was *right*. Despite all that we have discussed so far, it is possible to see a positive legacy from all the empires represented in Nebuchadnezzar's statue. For example, it is from Babylon that we receive some of our standard units of measurement - sixty seconds in a minute, sixty minutes in an hour, 24 hours in a day, 360 degrees in a circle.

Furthermore, many of the earliest advances in law, astronomy, mathematics, medicine and literature were made in Babylon. The oldest surviving legal code we have dates from around 1770 BC when Hammurabi was king of Babylon. Babylonian medicine pioneered the use of examination, diagnosis, prognosis and prescription. Literacy was high, and women as well as men learnt to read and write.

In astronomy the Babylonians charted the heavens extensively, tracking comets and eclipses as well as the motion of planets. Much later (around 150 BC) the Babylonian Seleucus was the first to suggest a universe of infinite scale, the first to suggest the moon as the cause of tides on earth, and the first to find independent evidence for Aristarchus' theory that the sun was the centre of the solar system.

The Jews also carried much of value back from Babylonia. One of their most famous Rabbis, Hillel, was a Babylonian Jew. It was from Babylon that the Jews brought synagogue worship back to Israel, along with a new alphabet (the square Hebrew characters that we recognise today). Aramaic, the language the

Jews acquired in Babylon, became the language of Jesus and later became the language of the Talmud, the principal compilation of which was written in Babylonia, not Jerusalem.

Furthermore, many Jews went back to Babylonia after they were expelled from Judea by Hadrian and remained there for centuries. Many achieved high positions under different regimes ruling the land: one, Sa'ad Al-Dawla, even became Chief Vizier of the Mongol Empire, the most powerful Jew since the time of Daniel. As recently as the 1920s, after the collapse of the Ottoman Empire, Baghdad still had a population that was 40% Jewish, who controlled 90% of the business.

The same positive comments could be made of Greek culture. It should not escape our attention that a huge proportion of the scientific and medical terms we use today have Greek roots. These are a by-product of the huge strides forward which the Greeks made in science, mathematics, architecture, deductive reasoning and philosophy, which took place alongside some very forward-thinking experiments with democracy. Athens in particular produced a remarkable flowering of culture under enlightened leaders such as Pericles between 460 and 430 BC. Like some of the Babylonian epics, Greek mythology also preserves stories that parallel some of those in the Old Testament (compare the story of Pandora with that of Eve or Orpheus and Eurydice with that of Lot and his wife).

Alexander the Great founded cities promulgating Greek culture and institutions wherever he went. The spread of Greek, as the common language of the Middle East for three centuries before Jesus, temporarily reversed the impact of Babel, and became the medium through which the New Testament was written and disseminated over a wide area.

Greek remained the language of the liturgy throughout the church until the 3rd Century AD when in the west it was gradually replaced by Latin, and even then the *Kyrie Eleison* ('Lord, have mercy') remained in Greek as part of the liturgy of the Catholic Church until the 1960s.

The stabilising influence provided by the Greek-speaking world was continued and extended by the Roman Empire. Augustine, in his epic work 'The City of God' later commented that 'the city of Rome was founded, like another Babylon ... by which God was pleased to conquer the whole world, and subdue it far and wide by bringing it into one fellowship of government and laws.'[1]

This wide reach of Roman imperial authority brought an unprecedented period of peace and security to the Mediterranean basin and far beyond. A marvellous network of roads underpinned by a strong military force made it possible to travel long distances by land or sea in relative safety, and a single system of justice prevailed throughout. Without the benefits of the *pax romana* and the speed of communication and transport that it produced, the gospel would have been unable to travel across the ancient world at the remarkable speed that it did. As a small memorial to this, we still remember Julius Caesar and the Emperor Augustus in our months of 'July' and 'August'.

The point in all these observations is that God's image within mankind was marred but not utterly destroyed by the fall. That image still shines even through our fallen nature and the rebellion of Babel and sparkles even through the imperfect aspirations of human civilisation.

This surviving afterglow of God's original purpose for man has sometimes been linked with a doctrine called 'common grace'. Even in our sinful state we still reflect something of God's likeness (Gen. 9.6, James 3.9) and God in turn continues to extend his broad, sustaining mercies to all of mankind, regardless of our response to him (Matt 5.45).

This is particularly apparent in the realm of human creativity. In chapter 1 of Genesis, for example, God organises and divides up what he has made through assigning names. In chapter 2, Adam, made in the image and likeness of God, is tasked with extending this work by tending the earth and creating names for the animals. This was part of mankind's primary commission and survives despite the fall. All our great achievements in language, music, science, law and commerce build on that initial instruction to categorise and label the things around us. By breaking reality into discrete, identifiable units we can then arrange and manipulate them in significant and beautiful ways.

Curiosity, research and creativity are thus vital aspects of being made in God's image. The book of Job reveals clearly this divine commission to seek out and discover:

> Mortals put an end to the darkness;
>   they search out the farthest recesses
>   for ore in the blackest darkness. ...
> People assault the flinty rock with their hands
>   and lay bare the roots of the mountains.
> They tunnel through the rock;
>   their eyes see all its treasures.
> They search the sources of the rivers
>   and bring hidden things to light. (Job 28.3, 9-11)

Even if Babylon was a distorted attempt to emulate the kingdom of God through man's own means, therefore, something of God's purposes still shines through. Each stage in the statue attempts to replicate in an imperfect way some aspect of the kingdom of God. When man works together for the common good, even in shameless self-advancement, good things can emerge even above faulty and corrupt foundations. Without Mussolini's Fascists and Hitler's Nazis, for example, we might not have motorways today.

In this sense all true scientific knowledge is ultimately a revelation from God, regardless of how it is discovered. Daniel reveals that God 'gives wisdom to the wise and knowledge to the discerning'; he 'reveals deep and hidden things' and 'knows what lies in darkness' (Dan. 2.21-22; see also Job 12.22). Proverbs reveals that 'the eyes of the LORD keep watch over knowledge' (22.12) and observes that while 'it is the glory of God to conceal a matter, to search out a matter is the glory of kings' (25.2). Colossians 2.3 reminds us that 'all the treasures of wisdom and knowledge' are hidden in Christ.

God has also made available sound principles of living to all mankind, regardless whether they know and acknowledge him or not (Prov. 8.4). Such wisdom underpins law, civilisation and prosperity and transcends all natural and religious boundaries. Indeed, many of the great 'wisdom' statements of the Bible have parallels in the sacred books of other religions, particularly the so-called 'Golden Rule' of Leviticus 19.18 and Matthew 22.39, which has close counterparts in Islam, Hinduism, Buddhism, Confucianism, Taoism and many other faiths. In his mercy God appears to have revealed aspects of his wisdom to all indiscriminately, regardless of race or creed, partly through the order inherent in the natural world (Rom.1.20). Jesus points out that 'even pagans' treat each other with civility (Matt. 5.47).

As examples of this, the priests of Dagon in Philistia seem to have a better understanding of God's ways than the Jewish priests (1 Sam. 2.12-17; 6.3-9); the sailors travelling to Tarshish seem to possess a deeper insight into God's heart than Jonah (Jonah 1.13-14), and the Roman centurion has a superior grasp of Jesus' authority than all the Jews living around him (Matt. 8.8-10). Paul writes that 'when Gentiles, who do not have the law, do by nature things required by the law, they are a law for themselves, even though they do not have the law. They show that the requirements of the law are written on their hearts, their consciences also bearing witness' (Rom. 2.14-15).

These universal principles of wisdom apply particularly in the realm of justice and good government (Prov. 8.14-16). Indeed, the qualities of a wise man described in Proverbs play a big part in defining the legacy and effectiveness of great leaders, whether or not they know God. Those who are honest, hard-working, generous, kind to the poor, even-tempered, refuse to take bribes and are ready to heed the advice of others are almost universally successful. Those, by contrast, who are dishonest, lazy, mean, cruel, easily angered, corrupt and unwilling to take counsel, are often authors of their own downfall.

As an example of this, Moses' father-in-law Jethro is able to offer him sound advice on delegation, even though he stands outside the Abrahamic covenant and appears to believe that Yahweh is just one of a multiplicity of gods (Ex. 18.11; 13-23). And in recent times we have seen the inspirational example of such men as Mahatma Gandhi, who, though not a Christian, was profoundly influenced by the ethical teaching of Jesus.[2]

Because they are divinely ordained, such principles of good and socially responsible government also have a positive impact on the wider populace, regardless of whether they have knowledge of God and his ways. In his commentary on the confusion of tongues at Babel, for instance, the first century Jewish writer Philo of Alexandria makes what is, from today's point of view, a far-sighted comment in this respect:

> But there are two kinds of cities, the one better, the other worse. The better kind enjoys a democratic government, [and] a constitution which honours equality, ruled by law and justice: such a constitution is a hymn to God. But the worse kind undermines this constitution ... through mob rule, which promotes inequality, in which injustice and lawlessness hold sway. Now good men are enrolled as citizens in the constitution of the first kind of city; but the multitude of the wicked clings to the other worst kind, loving disorder more than order, and confusion rather than well-established stability.[3]

Philo's understanding of the underlying principle of order and governance behind such enlightened rule was founded on the 'Logos', a term he borrowed from Greek philosophers such as Plato, and which shares some common ground with John's use of it in his gospel to describe Christ before his incarnation. Philo saw that this 'Logos' or 'Word' is reflected as much in human society as it is in the design of the universe and, as I have pointed out elsewhere, he anticipates many of the descriptions of Jesus that appear in the New Testament.[4] He even looked ahead to a time when, through the action of the 'Logos', democracy would spread throughout the entire world.[5]

If it is God who, through the eternal wisdom of his 'Logos', designs all these principles of order and social justice, it is also God who puts rulers and authorities in their place for his purposes to be outworked, however wicked or depraved some of them are (Dan. 2.37). Proverbs 21.1 says that 'In the LORD's hand the king's heart is a stream of water that he channels towards all who please him'.

This indiscriminate hand of providence through kings and leaders, often without any sense of awareness on their part, can be seen repeatedly throughout scripture. God used

Sennacherib without him knowing (Is. 37.26), describes Nebuchadnezzar as 'my servant' (Jer. 25.9; 27.6; 43.10), anoints Cyrus as his deliverer (Is. 45.1-6) and even speaks through Neco, king of Egypt (2 Chron. 35.21-22).

The same is true in the New Testament. Jesus says to Pilate that 'you would have no power over me if it were not given to you from above' (John 19.11). Paul reminds the Romans that 'there is no authority except that which God has established' (Rom 13.1).

It is also God who has established national boundaries and independent sovereign states over the course of history (Deut. 32.8); Paul declares that 'from one man he made all the nations, that they should inhabit the whole earth; and he marked out their appointed times in history and the boundaries of their lands' (Acts 17.26). These boundaries have helped to preserve the unique identity and languages of many people-groups, and will continue to exist at least in a remnant form in the new earth (Rev. 21.24-26; 22.2).

At the same time, God's purposes go beyond these divisions and the conflicts which they provoke (Is. 2.2-4). At different points in scripture we see visions of people-groups working together for the common good, a trend which reaches its climax in the vision of the great multitude 'from every nation, tribe, people and language' praising God in Revelation 7.9, an awe-inspiring picture of the universal church.

On a small scale, examples of such cross-cultural partnerships are apparent in the covenant of friendship that both Abraham and Isaac made with Abimelech, the leader of the Philistines (Gen. 21.27-31; 26.31), or in the friendship between David and the king of Moab, who offered shelter to him and his family after he fled from Saul (1 Sam. 22.3-4). On a national scale, we can see it in the alliance formed both by David and Solomon with Hiram, the Phoenician king of Tyre (2 Sam. 5.11; 1 Kings 5.1-12). And while Israel was often tempted to strike some very unhealthy bargains in her relationships with neighbouring states, incurring God's grave displeasure, recent history has amply demonstrated the value of her working together with reliable allies. It is questionable, for example, whether the modern state of Israel could have survived without the support of America and other sympathetic nations in the face of the barrage of hostility so often directed against her.

Can such coalitions work on a wider scale, or are they always doomed to fail under the weight of flawed human nature? Although, as we have noticed, national boundaries are God's own idea, many of the acute challenges that we face today, such as global pandemics, climate change, international terrorism or people trafficking have no respect for such frontiers. Under these circumstances it might seem natural for different countries to choose to act together to achieve certain goals. And at a time when nation so often rises against nation, as Jesus predicted (Matt. 24.7), the ministry of peace-making and reconciliation between peoples, a task clearly close to heart of God (Matt. 5.9; 2 Cor. 5.18-20), becomes ever more important.

For this reason, we should not necessarily see something sinister in the desire for a better world through enhanced global co-operation between nations. While many commentators sounding an alarm on this subject choose to focus on the demonically-controlled one-world government which will rule before Jesus returns, the Bible also describes an unparalleled period of global rule from Jerusalem under his kingship *after* he comes back. God has put eternity into the hearts of men (Ecc. 3.11), so it is natural that there should be an inner longing within the human psyche towards such a golden age, where conflicts are resolved and the earth is renewed, a hope that we can see expressed in writings stretching right back into antiquity.

It was this fundamental aspiration which drove Winston Churchill to declare, at the height of World War II, that

> we are also bound ... to look ahead to those days which will surely come when we shall have finally beaten down Satan under our feet and find ourselves with other great allies at once the masters and the servants of the future. ... We have learned from hard experience that stronger, more efficient, more rigorous world institutions must be created to preserve peace and to forestall the causes of future wars. In this task the strongest victorious nations must be combined, and also those who have borne the burden and heat of the day and suffered under the flail of adversity.[6]

For all their myriad imperfections, therefore, organisations such as the United Nations, and the League of Nations which preceded it, not only have a legitimate role to play, but may also reflect a wider subconscious human longing for the return of the Prince of Peace, when the wolf and lamb will dwell together (Is. 11.6; 65.25). It is perhaps significant that, outside the UN headquarters in New York, its founders placed the following inscription: 'they shall beat their swords into plowshares, and their spears into pruninghooks', taken from the description of end-time millennial age in Isaiah 2.4.[7]

At the same time, as we have observed in previous chapters, we should be acutely aware of hidden spiritual forces operating behind the scenes which also have a globalist agenda and are clearly trying to exploit some of these levers. Satan desires above all for the whole of humanity to bow before him (Matt.

4.8-9), and with that aim in mind is still seeking to push forward the original vision of Babel as a centralised one-nation, one-language, one-religion confederacy that will ultimately enable direct worship to him through his earthly representative (Rev. 13.4). Even back in Genesis 47.19-21 we see a bleak picture of a society towards the end of a 7-year period of tribulation in which an all-powerful state has taken control of everything and the entire population is working as slaves simply in order to eat. Could this provide a hint of what might lie in store in the future?

In order to establish such global rulership on a worldwide basis there will inevitably be a renewed push for the creation of a 'new world order'. Over the last century, many prominent figures have expressed support for such an idea, in which nation states might cede functions to a supranational body. The concept was initially floated after World War I by US President Woodrow Wilson, but later others such as H.G. Wells, Winston Churchill (as we have seen), Mikhail Gorbachev, George H. W. Bush and Tony Blair have jumped onto the bandwagon at different times. While many such desires spring from well-intentioned idealistic motives, Christians should treat them with the greatest of caution. We cannot ignore the fact that a time will come when world rulers will *voluntarily* confer their power on the 'beast' or antichrist, and a period of unparalleled central control of humanity and persecution against believers will begin (Rev. 13.7, 16-17; 17.13).

As believers, therefore, we need to be watchful, not allowing ourselves to be beguiled by every myth, fable and conspiracy theory that flies across the internet, but at the same time to remain alert to the times in which we are living. It is all the more important to be totally grounded in the truths of scripture, knowing that in all things God is totally in control and that everything will only happen at the time he allows.

For this reason, we should not be afraid or discouraged when wickedness and injustice prospers around us. The experience of Job reminds us that whatever disaster may befall us, God is still on the throne and works out all things for his own glory and the good of those who love him (Rom. 8.28). The key thing that matters ultimately is not where we are at the moment but how the story ends. All eyes must wait for the dramatic return of Jesus, to whom all history belongs, and which really is HIS STORY.

And it is the context of this story which must ultimately determine our understanding of great empires and civilisations, as well as the human institutions with which we have to deal on a daily basis. On the one hand we should applaud and celebrate all that is good, beautiful and uplifting in the secular world around us, and search for the hidden hand of God in every detail of human history and society. As Paul writes to the Philippian church:

> Whatever is true, whatever is noble, whatever is right, whatever is pure, whatever is lovely, whatever is admirable – if anything is excellent or praiseworthy – think about such things. (Phil. 4.8)

At the same time it is important to remember that the fundamental assumptions behind such attempts to create an earthly utopia are almost always wrong. The sin of Babylon was to misappropriate good principles as ends in themselves rather than to glorify God. On this account, we should not seek to whitewash the foundations of the Babylon system. For all its stunning achievements it is fundamentally rotten at the core, as chapters 17 and 18 of Revelation make clear.

Despite all that may lie ahead, however, we should be extremely thankful for the privilege of living in the times that we are now. It is so easy to become complacent and to forget that for many of us in the West we have riches and blessings that our distant ancestors could never even have imagined. We have electricity, clean water, advanced medical care, limitless travel possibilities, innumerable amazing gadgets and access to an unimaginable range of foodstuffs from across the world. We also have (for all its flaws) democratic government, a relatively impartial judicial system, and (despite steadily increasing restrictions) freedom of worship and expression.

We no longer have to cross the world to share the gospel with different people groups, because we can cross the street to do it. And within the comfort of our own homes, we can talk to someone on the other side of the world at the press of a button, watch outstanding concerts from the world's greatest performers, access vast libraries of information with a single click, or gaze at dramatic pictures of the landscape on Mars as if we were standing there ourselves.

All these things are the amazing by-products of 'common grace', through which God's purposes for man are still being worked out, even through the flawed constructs of human civilization. Even Solomon, in all his splendour, would be astonished at the everyday resources and possibilities available to us today that we all too easily take for granted.

And yet, for Christians, what we experience now is just the merest drop in the ocean compared with the glory that awaits us. As Paul writes, 'No eye has seen, no ear has heard, and no mind has imagined what God has prepared for those who love him' (1 Cor. 2.9 NLT, quoting from Isaiah 64.4). 'For now we see only a reflection as in a mirror; then we shall see face to face. Now I know in part; then I shall know fully, even as I am fully known.' (13.12). All the marvels around us now pale into insignificance compared to the wonders that lie ahead.

Whatever our lot in this world, therefore, there is good news for us. However tough things may be for us right now, relief is on its way. But conversely, even if things are going well, we know that there is something unimaginably better still to come.

Questions to Consider:

(i)   What positive things can we see in the culture around us? To what extent do non-Christians put us to shame, and how can we learn from the example of others with different worldviews and apply the lessons in our own lives?

(ii)   Read Nehemiah 2.1-20. Why was it important for him to secure the king's covering and authorisation to rebuild Jerusalem? What are the damaged walls that we need to repair in our lives and where are the broken walls in our nation and our world?

(iii)   What are the advantages of countries working together and what are the limitations? Is it beneficial for nations to pool sovereignty or are there dangers? Are there circumstances where it is better for a country to resist the collective will of others and to strike out on its own?

---

12 THE LIGHTS OF THE METROPOLIS

If there is one song more than any other that seems to bring alive the spirit of the 1960s, it is 'Downtown'. Composed by Tony Hatch and sung by the young Petula Clark, it seems to convey the hope that the bustle of city life can be a panacea to all the world's problems:

When you're alone and life is making you lonely
You can always go downtown;
When you've got worries, all the noise and the hurry
Seems to help, I know, downtown.

Just listen to the music of the traffic in the city,
Linger on the sidewalk where the neon signs are pretty,
How can you lose?
The lights are much brighter there,
You can forget all your troubles, forget all your cares,

So go downtown,
Things will be great when you're downtown,
No finer place for sure, downtown,
Everything's waiting for you.

For all their problems, cities manage to convey a tremendous sense of optimism and hope. From the Greek and Latin roots of the word 'city' we get such words as 'civil', 'civilised', 'urbane' and 'polite'. There is a fascination with sound and brightness in the song, and the blaze of lights along with the upward thrust of skyscrapers is a marked feature of almost every major modern city in the world today.

As we have seen, the climax of the Bible is the triumphant descent of the heavenly city, the New Jerusalem, from heaven to earth, illuminated in eternal daytime (Rev. 21.2; 23-25). Everything within the human psyche longs for this moment, where we can indeed, as Petula Clark sings, 'forget all our troubles, forget all our cares'. Every human aspiration for the grandeur and brilliance of the city reflects an instinctive desire to capture this within our own time. God has set that longing for a heavenly city in our own hearts.

In this sense, however marred by human pride and vain ambition, the aspirations behind the New Jerusalem are woven deep into the human consciousness, and extend back to the very dawn of human history. Just as Adam was assigned to tend and order the garden where God placed him, so his descendants have sought to apply God-given principles of order to the human environment around them. Planned, grid-like systems appear in cities over many widely-separated parts of the world throughout history, from Teotihuacan in Mexico to Chengzhou in China, and from Mohenjo-Daro in India back in 2500 BC, to Milton Keynes in our own day.

For example, like the New Jerusalem, Chengzhou was designed as a square lined on an exact north-south axis with three gates on each side of the city. We also noted in an earlier chapter that, under the rulership of Nebuchadnezzar, Babylon was rebuilt as a perfect square, 120 stadia in length on each side, a remarkable anticipation of the measurements of the New Jerusalem (12,000 stadia in each side), with the Euphrates flowing through the very heart of the city (compare Genesis 2:10-14 and Revelation 22:1-2).

The Greeks and Romans exported these grid patterns on a massive scale. Indeed the Romans often used identical street patterns in their military garrisons, with every building reproduced in exactly the same position, so that soldiers posted to a different location in the empire would often find themselves quartered at addresses identical to where they had been before.

The fascination with light in our cities today also seems to look forward to the fulfilment of the heavenly vision at the end of Revelation. John, who saw it, would doubtless have been familiar with Harbour Street in Ephesus, with its 50 huge lights carved into the marble along a colonnaded avenue 580 yards long and 12 yards wide, one of just three streets in the Roman Empire to have public street lights (the other two being in Rome and Antioch). But doubtless these would have paled into insignificance compared to the non-stop illumination of the heavenly city, with its great central street, and the crystal-clear river of the water of life running along the middle (Rev. 21.23-25, 22.1-2,5).

The desire in cities to build *upwards* is also an anticipation of the New Jerusalem, which rises as high as it spreads out in width. The relentless upward thrust has been a mark of cities from Babel onwards, almost like artificial mountain ranges designed to project power. The very word 'skyscraper' is reminiscent of a legend in the Jewish Talmud where the builders of the tower of Babel were motivated by an attempt to pierce a hole in the firmament of heaven.[2]

In some cases, these towers may have originated from an attempt to placate the gods. For instance, the Sumerians, the ancient inhabitants of Mesopotamia, believed that gods lived on mountaintops. The built ziggurats as artificial mountains so that their gods could descend from heaven and dwell there. As with the frequent alignment of cities on precise north-south axes, the underlying motivation was thus often spiritual or occultic in origin. The literal meaning of 'Babel' was *Bab-El* ('gateway of God').

Indeed, not content with cities that merely *reach* the heavens, like Babel, some have aspired in our own day to build cities *in* the heavens. While the floating city of Laputa in Jonathan Swift's *Gulliver's Travels* in 1726 was a tongue-in-cheek dig at the scientific elite of his time, several serious suggestions for cities in orbit around earth or in the upper atmosphere of Venus have surfaced over the last fifty years, while the entrepreneur Elon Musk has declared his intention to build a city of one million inhabitants on Mars by 2050.[1]

Such bold ambitions might suggest that, as with Babel, a stronger motivation for the design of cities seems to be human pride and prestige. 'Let us make a name *for ourselves*,' its builders declare boldly. And it seems significant that whenever Babylon is mentioned in the Bible, this same thrusting upward image recurs over and over again. The king of Babylon desires to 'ascend above the tops of the clouds' to make himself like the Most High (Is. 14.14). Babylon is a destroying mountain (Jer. 51.25) whose judgement reaches to the skies (51.9). 'Even if Babylon reaches the sky and fortifies her lofty stronghold, I will send destroyers against her' (51.53). Her sins are 'piled high as the heavens' (Rev. 18.5).

Indeed, it seems to have been the *height* of the cities in Canaan that was a particular deterrent to the spies who were sent into the Promised Land. In Numbers 13.28 they report back that 'the cities are fortified and very large' while in the account in Deuteronomy 1.28, the words are 'the cities are large, with *walls up to the sky*,' using the same Hebrew phrase that appears in the Babel account in Genesis 11.4. An identical expression appears in Deuteronomy 9.1, again focusing on the powerful challenge of the cities to be conquered.

Although we generally consider high-rise apartments to be exclusively a feature of modern life, blocks of up to ten storeys were not uncommon in ancient Rome and other major cities of the empire. The Roman poet Martial, in his *Epigrams,* describes an avid but over-indulgent food connoisseur who has to climb two hundred stairs every night to reach his apartment.[3] There were, of course, no lifts in those days, so he must have burnt up a good few calories from each meal with every ascent!

Later such buildings became notable across parts of the Islamic world. Fustat, the one-time capital of Egypt, contained high-rise residential buildings able to accommodate hundreds of people. An 11th century writer described some of them rising up to 14 storeys, with roof gardens on the top irrigated by ox-drawn water wheels.[4] In our own day the colossal structure of the Burj Khalifa in Dubai far exceeds anything else in the world, and in its steely optimism might be seen as a modern-day equivalent of the tower of Babel. The nation which hosts it, the United Arab Emirates, has also declared, like Elon Musk, a city on Mars as its next step forward.[5]

Our modern fascination with the skyscraper might remind us of a second dream which Nebuchadnezzar has in Daniel chapter 4, which portrays him as a personification of Babylon itself: he is a 'tree in the middle of the land' whose 'height was enormous' and 'visible to the ends of the earth' so that 'its top touched the sky' (v. 11). Its fate, like Babel, or the ill-fated Twin Towers in New York in our own day, was to be cut down to a stump, a personal warning to Nebuchadnezzar as to what was about to happen in his own life (vv. 20-27). It is a symbolic reminder to us that, at the return of Jesus, every 'mountain and hill' of human vanity will be laid low, and his name exalted far above all (Is. 2.2; 40.4; Phil. 2.9-11).

If the upward vision of Babel and its premature attempt to unify mankind independently of God backfired in a catastrophic manner, producing a fracturing of languages, cultures and beliefs, there was an interesting by-product. Multiculturalism and pluralism became hallmarks of major international cities from an early age. They became home to an increasingly wide share of languages and people-groups. It is interesting to note, for example, that the tree we have just described in Nebuchadnezzar's second dream seems to represent a meeting-place for very culture and nationality, a feature of Babylon and the empires which succeeded it: 'under it the wild animals found shelter, and the birds lived in its branches; from it every creature was fed' (Dan. 4.12).

The result of this growing diversity was not just a melting-pot of races and languages, but a marketplace of faiths. In a polytheistic system where many gods exist, it was never difficult to add a few more.

This trend continued with the empires that followed on from Babylon. Alexander's conquests exposed the Greek world to a range of beliefs from Babylonia, Persia and Egypt. Later Roman conquests made these available to an even wider audience. While this greater awareness of other languages, cultures and faiths at variance from the majority sometimes resulted in persecution, more often it produced a 'live-and-let-live' tolerance. Ezra 7.23 shows that the Persian emperor's open-mindedness sprang from a desire to placate all gods. Which way was the right way? Here perhaps is the background to Pilate's famous exclamation 'What is truth?' that we discussed in Chapter Ten.

Indeed, the Roman Empire was marked by an extraordinary degree of toleration of different beliefs. Until Christianity was effectively outlawed by the emperor Nero the only religion the Romans had ever proscribed completely was Druidism, because of its practice of human sacrifice.

This may go some way towards explaining why city-dwellers, exposed to a variety of opinions, people-groups and faiths, have generally been more progressive and tolerant in their outlook. This was apparent even within Judaism. In the time of Jesus, for example, there were two main schools of Pharisees: the followers of Shammai who were more conservative and unyielding in their belief-system, and who were concentrated in the countryside, and those of Hillel who were more generous-spirited, pragmatic and accommodating towards the Roman authorities, and who were more dominant in the towns.

In modern times this also seems to be true. In the referendum in 2016 in Britain there was a significant discrepancy between the voting patterns of larger cities and smaller provincial towns. In general, large metropolitan areas voted against Brexit. Educated metropolitan elites have traditionally supported liberal values and globalisation and have spearheaded 'progressive' social reform, but often at the expense of traditional Christian and Biblical values.

This cultural divide between city dwellers and country dwellers in their attitudes towards variety and diversity is also apparent in the realm of commerce, and goes way back to the dawn of history. These two sets of values arose from two fundamentally different modes of living.

In traditional rural societies, everything - clothes, furniture, building materials - was harvested and put together from scratch at source. There was a direct connection between land and artefact and the scope for choice or variation was extremely limited.

As agriculture became more efficient, however, millions were released from a lifestyle of dependency on the seasons and the unpredictable fluctuations of weather to settle in cities. No longer relying on divine providence, they began to rely on human ingenuity in craft, trade and finance. As a result, cities became centres of great human achievement and learning, as well as trade.

No longer tied to the productivity of the land, goods needed to be bartered or purchased through another means of exchange. In essence this explains the origins of the financial system. It became possible to make choices as to *what* to purchase and therefore diversification and competition arose. Gradually a bewildering variety of options became available. 'The more goods there are, the more people there are to consume them' (Ecc. 5.11, *The Voice*). Ezekiel 16.29 describes Babylonia as 'a land of merchants'. Even sex became a commodity to be marketed.

All of these developments brought challenges of their own. With more and more people concentrated in ever smaller areas, problems such as congestion, social inequality, overcrowding, poor sanitation and infectious diseases became increasingly problematic and have remained a perennial scourge of city life to this day.

Under these circumstances the need to plan, unify, organise and connect also becomes ever greater. This has always been a driving vision for city planners. Organised grid-like street plans have a long history, as we have already seen. But all too often it is an outwardly imposed, cosmetic unity that fails to stifle alienation and social division. Modernism in the 1960s was often driven by utopian visions of 'towers in parkland' but redevelopment in many British cities has proved to be a disaster, and cost civic authorities many millions in bulldozing and starting again from scratch. In recent times the memory of the Grenfell fire is still sharply etched on our consciousness.

The vision behind such developments has far too often been an inflexible, controlling one. We noted earlier how the Romans rolled out town plans that were carbon copies of each other across the whole of the empire, imposing an unyielding conformity to a central vision. Likewise, Rabbi Allen Maller has suggested that an equally mechanistic view of society may have motivated the original vision behind Babel. Pointing out how baking hundreds of thousands of bricks for such huge building projects would have produced the first mass production factories, he comments that they wanted to build their city with uniform manufactured bricks, instead of natural unhewn stones. They did not want each stone to be a different shape and colour from all the other stones because they wanted to unify themselves by highly organized, conformist, teamwork, factory behaviour, as well as an all-encompassing common purpose. ... Their plan for the city might have been modelled on bee hives or termite mounds: lots of close contact, with a high degree of conformity.[6]

There is a lesson to be learnt here, as can be seen from the drab processions of forbidding socialist-era blocks that mar so many cities in Eastern Europe. A happy city comes from ordered hearts, not ordered buildings, however appealing these might seem to look on paper. Outwardly imposed design and unity cannot atone for or repair the brokenness in our relationships caused by the fall.

If many of the goals of town planning arise from a (sometimes misplaced) desire to unify and connect, the same has been evident in the social sphere, as individuals have banded together to influence the levers of commerce and power. From the earliest times onwards, guilds, craft organisations and other human networks became vehicles through which citizens could exert influence by working together (an example can be seen in Acts 19.24-27). Some of these were open and legal with honourable intentions; others were little more than criminal gangs extorting money or warring for prestige and control.

As communications have improved throughout history, such networks have developed in extent and complexity. The rapid growth of the church in the first century AD, aided by the ease of travel within the Roman Empire, shows how quickly ideas can spread and interlock. At the same time, however, all kinds of clandestine societies, organised crime networks and government spy rings have also sprung up in the shadows over the centuries, hidden under the cloak of secrecy. And as the world has been criss-crossed by ever-increasing trade activity, multinational conglomerates and banking institutions have developed, touching all corners of the earth.

Today Babylon has interlocked the world as a *global* city held together by social, financial and information networks (Facebook, Google and many more). Together with the connected devices of television, GPS, mobile phones, a virtual banking system, and the so-called 'internet of things', it has created an *omniscience* and *omnipresence* which, joined up with other technological and scientific advances, offer a kind of *omnipotence*. In our own time the original vision for Babel, to unite everything under a single banner in place of God, has truly come of age.

We are close to the state that Babylon has reached in the Book of Revelation before its sudden demise. She is a truly global city that 'rules over the kings of the earth' (17.18), and is 'seated on many waters' (17.1 ESV) with authority over 'peoples, multitudes, nations and languages' (17.15). She has become a massive trade and financial hub (18.11-19), a playground for the rich (18.3) and an influential cultural and manufacturing centre (18.22). Yet she conceals many dark secrets: gross immorality (17.5), human trafficking (18.13) and the cold-blooded murder of God's people (18.24). Above all she is preoccupied with herself, seemingly unassailable in her apparent omnipotence (18.7).

Today's cities reflect many of the aspirations of the original builders of Babel. We have interlinked the world with vast information networks. We have literally reached the heavens with satellites (used for TV, phone and GPS). And we scour the universe for some other pulsation of life, desperate to drive another nail into the coffin of the idea of a special creation or a privileged role of man that might reinstate God to his true position. By our technology, driven by IT, and our mythology, driven by ET, we are effectively worshipping the universe rather than the Creator.

We saw in the last chapter how Paul warns in chapter 1 of his letter to the Romans of the results that proceed from worshipping and serving created things: moral degradation that ultimately provokes the wrath of God. Like Babylon, the end result is our holding a golden cup, beautiful on the outside but filled with abominable things and the filth of our adulteries (Rev. 17.4). The end result is sheer brokenness and futility, as we reap the bitter consequences. It may not be a coincidence that the first city to be described in any detail in scripture is Sodom.

Behind the bright and comforting neon lights of downtown, therefore, a very different reality is exposed. All our attempts to stifle the pain inside us with technology and pleasure are ultimately hollow. As physical health has improved, mental health has deteriorated. The end-results are a breakdown of the individual, the family and of society. We have reaped the same judgement that fell first on Eden and then on Babel - more and more disharmony within, disharmony with God, disharmony in society, and disharmony with nature. Divorce, depression, self-harm, suicide, abortion and addiction run rife in our streets and homes. Despair is written across many of our cities and no quantity of glittering lights can dispel it.

With our fractured cities crying out under the weight of family breakdown, addiction, gang warfare, knife crime, and intense loneliness and alienation, the need for the gospel to reach out and transform has never been greater. We need an urgent vision and strategy to reach different ethnic groups, age groups and social classes, and be ready to commandeer all the resources of social media, compassionate engagement as well as mass evangelism strategies.

Most of all, we need to learn to work together in unity, across denominations and doctrinal divides. This is a genuine oneness that only God can bestow, in contrast to the artificial oneness of Babel. Psalm 133 reminds us, 'How good and pleasant it is when God's people live together in unity ... for there the LORD bestows his blessing, even life for evermore. (v. 1,3). Likewise Proverbs tells us that 'when the righteous prosper, the city rejoices ... through the blessing of the upright a city is exalted' (11.10-11).

Right now, the fields are ripe for harvest. We must seize the opportunity to reach out while the doors still remain open to us. Just as Jesus wept over Jerusalem, God calls us to cry out over our cities today, that his kingdom might come and his will be done. Let us ask the Lord of the harvest, therefore, to send out workers into his harvest field (Luke 10.2) and to be ready to be part of the answer ourselves. Ultimately, just as he is the light of the New Jerusalem, it is *us* who he is calling to be the lights of the earthly metropolis (Matt. 5.14-16).

Questions to Consider:

(i)   Much of Paul's work was done in cities. Why was this? What social networks and community projects can we harness and exploit to shine the light of God's kingdom to those in brokenness and despair?

(ii)   Read chapters 3 and 4 of Jonah. Why was Jonah reluctant to preach to Nineveh? (Compare Nahum 3.1-7). How did the city react? Given this response, was Jonah expecting his original prophecy still to be fulfilled afterwards, and what insight does this give into his personality (4.5)? How do we react when God prompts us to share the good news outside our normal comfort zones?

(iii)   In the New Jerusalem, nothing impure is to be brought into the city from outside (Rev. 21.27) and the leaves of the tree of life bring healing to the nations (22.2). How can we reflect this in our thinking and speaking, and model it in our own homes and to the communities around us? (Consider also Deut. 7.26; Eph. 4.25-5.4; Prov. 12.18-19; 15.4; 18.20-21).

13 BABYLON IN THE HEART

Up to now, we have spent considerable time considering two external forces battling against each other in the world around us. It is a conflict that has shaped the course of history, and it will continue to mould our destiny in a powerful way.

Against this background the temptation to identify modern 'Babylon' with particular institutions such as the UN, the EU or the Vatican is naturally very enticing. But this kind of scapegoating, though understandable, somehow misses the point, even where strong correlations might seem to exist. We are dealing here with *spiritual* strongholds, not with external human organisations as such.

Jesus was once asked a similar question about the kingdom of God by those seeking to pin it down to a particular place and time. His reply is illuminating:

> 'The Kingdom of God isn't ushered in with visible signs. You won't be able to say, "It has begun here in this place or there in that part of the country." *For the Kingdom of God is within you.*' (Luke 17.20-21 NLT)

This points us to a key essential truth. The main stronghold of Babylon is not hidden in the corridors of power but is locked away deep inside the human heart. We can never fully understand how the Babylon spirit operates in the world unless we gain insight into how it works within each one of us.

In his letter to the Romans Paul spends a considerable time discussing the struggle that takes place in our hearts on a daily basis. The same fundamental forces and motivations are at work within us that we see in the wider world, but they are described using different terms. Paul describes them as the 'flesh' (or 'old nature') versus the Spirit.

A veiled anticipation of this inner conflict can be seen in Genesis chapter 25. Rebekah has conceived and is expecting twins, but the babies jostle each other within her (v.22):

> The LORD said to her,
> 'Two nations are in your womb,
>   and two peoples from within you will be separated;
> one people will be stronger than the other,
>   and the elder will serve the younger.' (v.23)

This picture offers a profound insight as to what happens in the heart of the believer. There is a battle raging within us between polar opposites. The flesh not only *does* not submit to God, but it *cannot* (Rom. 8.7). Paul writes that 'For the desires of the flesh are against the Spirit, and the desires of the Spirit are against the flesh, for these are opposed to each other, to keep you from doing the things you want to do.' (Gal. 5.17 ESV)

This is a reminder to us that man's fallen way of thinking is the diametric opposite of God's way of thinking. Even our best motives in the natural get puffed up with pride. After Jesus has commended Simon Peter for acknowledging him as the Messiah in Mark's gospel, he goes on to talk about what that

Messiahship really entails. Far from being the glorious reign of triumph that his disciples were expecting, it was to be a tortuous road leading to the agonies of the cross. Peter, now doubtless feeling a few feet taller in stature after Jesus' words of blessing, begins to remonstrate with him.

Jesus' reply is stern and uncompromising: "Get behind me, Satan. You are thinking not as God does, *but as human beings do*" (Mark 8.33 NAB).

Satan is utterly opposed to everything in the kingdom of God. And yet he comes knocking as a visitor that we choose to entertain all too often, to disastrous effect (2 Sam. 12.4). Our mind is a citadel which he attempts to capture (Acts 5.3), our heart is a doorway that he attempts to harden (Eph. 4.18) and our eyes are windows that he attempts to blind (2 Cor. 4.4).

The root problem which allows him a foothold, of course, is a three-letter word with 'I' in the middle of it. **Sin** gets between us and God and thus creates a vacuum that the powers of darkness can fill. Like a virus, it seeks to infect us and turn us into a host through which it can transmit its poison to others. It battles against us (Heb. 12.4; 1 Pet. 2.11), turns us into slaves (John 8.34; Romans 6.16), imprisons us (Prov. 5.22; Ecc. 8.8), takes over control of our mind (Rom. 7.20, 23, 2 Pet. 2.19) and seeks to prevent us from returning to God (Prov. 2.19; Hos. 5.4).

The Bible treats sin as a deadly toxic substance that needs to be disposed of carefully, almost like radioactive waste (Lev. 16.21-22). As we know, like a tiny speck of plutonium, it only takes a tiny trace of evil to contaminate anything that is good. One droplet of sin is enough to ruin our lives (Matt. 5.22,28; James 2.10) and lead us on a slow and agonising march towards destruction (Prov. 14.12; Rom. 6.23).

We are faced, then, with what is literally a life-or-death struggle. This is the warning that God gave to Cain: 'Sin is crouching at the door, eager to control you. But you must subdue it and be its master.' (Gen 4.7 NLT)'.

As in any battle, we need a strategy. Since sin has a life-cycle (Eph. 4.18-19; James 1.14-15) it is all the more important to destroy it while it is young. We need to dig up the roots below as well as the fruits above (Amos 2.9). Digging up small weeds with a trowel is far easier than attempting to tear down fully-grown shrubs with a heavy-duty strimmer, where what lies below the surface continues to remain potent and undisturbed.

Uprooting the poisonous shoots of sin, therefore, needs to be an ongoing practice in our lives on a daily basis (Matthew 15.13). We are called to 'trample on snakes and scorpions and to overcome all the power of the enemy' (Luke 10.19), to 'demolish arguments and every pretension that sets itself up against the knowledge of God', and 'to take captive every thought to make it obedient to Christ' (2 Cor. 10.5).

Of course, this is a battle that we have no hope whatsoever of winning in our own strength. The odds stacked against us are impossibly steep. Without the power of God's Spirit we are doomed to keep trudging round in endless circles, as pitifully outlined in the book of Judges. And any breakthroughs that we do achieve on our own simply generate a flurry of pride, enabling a Babel-like tower of self-righteousness to rise up within us.

Paul describes the sheer futility of this struggle more fully in chapter 7 of Romans:

> For if I know the law but still can't keep it, and if the power of sin within me keeps sabotaging my best intentions, I obviously need help! I realize that I don't have what it takes. I can will it, but I can't do it. I decide to do good, but I don't

really do it; I decide not to do bad, but then I do it anyway. My decisions, such as they are, don't result in actions. Something has gone wrong deep within me and gets the better of me every time.

It happens so regularly that it's predictable. The moment I decide to do good, sin is there to trip me up. I truly delight in God's commands, but it's pretty obvious that not all of me joins in that delight. Parts of me covertly rebel, and just when I least expect it, they take charge.

I've tried everything and nothing helps. I'm at the end of my rope. Is there no one who can do anything for me? Isn't that the real question? (Rom. 7.17-24, *The Message*)

The wonderful news of the gospel is that God has provided us with the perfect answer. Since our sin is infinite in God's sight (Ezra 9.6; Job 22.5 KJV) and is directed first and foremost against an infinite being (Ps. 51.4) only God himself can put it right. As 'no one can redeem the life of another or give to God a ransom for them' (Ps. 49.7) it is he alone who has to step in and do the work himself (49.15; Is. 59.16).

The answer to God's challenge to Cain to 'win against sin' is, therefore, to be found in Christ, the Word made flesh, who alone, as 'God with us', can offer that infinite life on our behalf (Heb. 7.16). Since there is no forgiveness of sins without the shedding of blood, it is only through the blood sacrifice of Jesus on the cross that we are set free (Heb. 9.11-15, 22). In him that dominion of sin is completely removed (John 8.36; Rom. 6.14) so that we might have life to the full (John 10.10).

Furthermore, because the life that Jesus offered was infinite, the consequences of that sacrifice are infinite. 'He is able to save *to the uttermost* those who draw near to God through him' (Heb. 7.25 ESV). 'For by one sacrifice he has *made perfect for ever* those who are being made holy.' (Heb. 10.14) The cross puts everything into reverse and turns the life-cycle of ever-increasing sin into a life-cycle of exponentially increasing righteousness (Rom. 6.19).

The great key that unlocks all of these extraordinary blessings is faith. And yet faith is one of the world's most misunderstood concepts. It is not a virtue that we add to our Christian life. It is, rather, an acknowledgment of our total insufficiency and powerlessness in the face of sin, and our need to rely wholly on the sufficiency and power of God.

Paul's discussion of the power of faith in his letter to the Galatians rests on his use of a verse from Habakkuk. In its original context this shows how faith is the opposite of human pride:

> Look at the proud! Their spirit is not right in them, but the righteous live by their faith. (Hab. 2.4 NRSV)

It is so easy for us to fall into the trap of thinking that our actions place God under an obligation to us. In actual fact, the opposite is the case. We do not receive righteousness through relying on God's law, but through relying on *him* alone, who *is* our righteousness. Faith therefore places no trust in anything within ourselves, but yields a total surrender to God and his infinite provision. Far from being rooted in pride, it is tied to humility and an acceptance of our own powerlessness to change without Christ.

In this sense faith is the polar opposite of the Babylon principle, where man places himself at the top and trusts in his own actions alone. Everything in the kingdom of God is an inversion of world's way of doing things. With religion everything is done *by* us. With God everything is done *to* us.

Paul contrasts these two ways of thinking graphically in his letter to the Philippians:

If someone else thinks they have reasons to put confidence in the flesh, I have more: circumcised on the eighth day, of the people of Israel, of the tribe of Benjamin, a Hebrew of Hebrews; in regard to the law, a Pharisee; as for zeal, persecuting the church; as for righteousness based on the law, faultless.

But whatever were gains to me I now consider loss for the sake of Christ. What is more, I consider everything a loss because of the surpassing worth of knowing Christ Jesus my Lord, for whose sake I have lost all things. I consider them garbage, that I may gain Christ and be found in him, not having a righteousness of my own that comes from the law, but that which is through faith in Christ – the righteousness that comes from God on the basis of faith. (Phil. 3.4-9)

We have already seen how Pentecost is a reversal of Babel, man's attempt to reach God through his own efforts and through external means. While Babel reaches upwards, God comes *down* through his Spirit at Pentecost. Everything under the new covenant follows this top-down pattern. We are born *from above* (John 3.3,7); the veil in the temple is torn *from top to bottom* (Matt. 27.51); Jesus promises we will be 'clothed with power *from on high*' (Luke 24.49); the sailsheet in Acts is *lowered from heaven* (Acts 10.11); the New Jerusalem *descends from heaven to earth* in Revelation (21.2).

Many of us have been labouring all night in the fruitless battle of unaided human effort, but have reaped nothing except frustration and discouragement. Jesus is calling us to cast our net on the other side, and allow *him* to do all the work. Babel was constructed out of man-made bricks (Gen. 11.3-4), but God required that his altars be built from unhewn stones (Ex. 20.25). We can either have religion or God, but we cannot have both.

In this sense, faith is the great leveller - through the cross all are equal in God's sight, from the richest businessman to the

145

poorest beggar. Our model is not to emulate the great and the mighty. Instead we are to pattern ourselves on little children, out of whose mouths God has brought forth powerful praise (Ps. 8.2). As Jesus reminds us,

> Truly I tell you, unless you change and become like little children, you will never enter the kingdom of heaven. Therefore, whoever takes the lowly position of this child is the greatest in the kingdom of heaven. And whoever welcomes one such child in my name welcomes me.'
>
> (Matt.18. 3-5)

This child-like dependence of faith is all God's work, from start to finish. There is always a temptation to think that there is something that we can bring to the table, for which we can take a modicum of credit. But even our faith itself is God's free gift to us (Eph. 2.8).

The Bible likens our own unaided efforts to yeast, which works invisibly within a substance to change it into something else. Jesus warned his disciples to 'be on your guard against the yeast of the Pharisees and Sadducees' who thought their good works could earn favour with God (Matt. 16.6-11). And Paul, when arguing against attempts to add circumcision to the finished work of the cross, said similarly that 'a little yeast works through the whole batch of dough' (Gal. 5.9).

The simple truth is that there is nothing extra that we can add to our faith (Gal. 5.2-6), nothing we can add to the cross (Gal. 6.14), nothing we can add to the new birth (Gal. 6.15), nothing we can add to the gospel (Gal. 1.6-9), nothing we can add to the Bible (Rev. 22.18-19), nothing we can add to our prayers (Luke 18.9-14), nothing we can add in the healing ministry (Acts 3.12), and nothing we can add to a genuine move of God

(Ecc. 3.14). All is complete in Christ and all stands or falls in him.

Religion is addictive. Like Babel it is never finished, as there is always another rung to the ladder which needs to be added to reach a heaven that appears to recede further and further into the distance. Like sin, these unreachable demands impose a harsh servitude on us (Ex. 6.9). In Christ, by contrast, that ladder is already complete, and we can rest in his finished work which spans the entire gulf between earth and heaven (compare John 1.51 with Genesis 28.12).

In Galatians Paul makes a contrast between this slavery to religion and the true freedom available to us in Christ, likening it to the contrast between earthly Jerusalem and the heavenly Jerusalem, which we have already seen gloriously portrayed at the end of Revelation:

> Tell me, you who want to be under the law, are you not aware of what the law says? For it is written that Abraham had two sons, one by the slave woman and the other by the free woman. His son by the slave woman was born according to the flesh, but his son by the free woman was born as the result of a divine promise.
>
> These things are being taken figuratively: the women represent two covenants. One covenant is from Mount Sinai and bears children who are to be slaves: this is Hagar. Now Hagar stands for Mount Sinai in Arabia and corresponds to the present city of Jerusalem, because she is in slavery with her children. But the Jerusalem that is above is free, and she is our mother. For it is written:
>
> 'Be glad, barren woman,
>   you who never bore a child;
> break forth and cry aloud,
>   you who were never in labour;
> because more are the children of the desolate woman
>   than of her who has a husband.' (Gal. 4.21-27)

In English there are two meanings for the word 'yield'. The first means to surrender or give way. The second means to bear fruit. In the Bible, the two meanings overlap. You can't have one without the other. Only when we 'yield' in the first sense, by ceasing to try and 'earn' favour with God, can we 'yield' in the second. Jesus reminds us that 'I am the vine; you are the branches. If you remain in me and I in you, you will bear much fruit; apart from me you can do nothing' (John 15.5).

Faith, then, is a turning away from our own works towards a simple trust in God, against everything the enemy can throw at it. It is the ability to sleep in the boat through the midst of the storm (Mark 4.38).

Over and over again the Bible shows us what this child-like 'yielding' or 'remaining' looks like in practice:

> 'Do not be afraid. Stand firm and you will see the deliverance the LORD will bring you today. ... The LORD will fight for you; you need only to be still.' (Ex. 14.13-14)

> 'Now then, stand still and see this great thing the LORD is about to do before your eyes!' (1 Sam. 12.16)

> 'You will be delivered by returning and resting; your strength will lie in quiet confidence.' (Is. 30.15 HCSB)

> 'You will not need to fight in this battle; take your position, stand still, and see the victory of the LORD on your behalf, O Judah and Jerusalem.' (2 Chron. 20.17 RSV)

Yet, despite this deep quietness in trust, there is also an active aspect to it. It is a determination to push through against all the odds. We see powerfully spelt out in the 'hall of fame' in Hebrews chapter 11 where so many heroes of the faith are commended for their grit and perseverance without ever seeing the results for themselves:

These were all commended for their faith, yet none of them received what had been promised, since God had planned something better for us so that only together with us would they be made perfect. (Heb. 11.39-40)

It is this dogged determination to push through despite everything thrown against us that marks the essence of a victorious, faith-filled life. Faced with every misfortune possible, Job is still adamant that '*even if* he slays me, I will hope in him' (Job 13.15 NET). Similarly Shadrach, Meshach and Abednego, threatened by Nebuchadnezzar with being thrown into the blazing furnace for not worshipping the idolatrous statue, are confident that

'the God we serve is able to deliver us from it, and he will deliver us from Your Majesty's hand. But *even if he does not*, we want you to know, Your Majesty, that we will not serve your gods or worship the image of gold you have set up.'

(Dan. 3.17-18)

We need to be ruthless, then, in pulling down the idols of power, money, greed, sex and success which are attempting to suffocate us (Rom. 8.13). Our hearts are God's sanctuary, and there should be room for nothing else. Winning over the Promised Land of our souls requires determination, and there should be no place for compromise with the forces that seek to destroy us from within. Failure to do so comprehensively may leave us with a 'thorn in the side' which risks becoming a constant stumbling block in our Christian walk (Num. 33.55).

A popular acronym for 'faith' is '**F**orsaking **A**ll **I T**rust **H**im'. It presents a powerful challenge. Are we willing to forsake all for Jesus, despite the cost? Are we willing to trust him with everything? Are we willing to lay down our lives for him?

Jesus's question to his disciples, 'Who do you say that I am?' is therefore one that is directed to every single one of us today. What is our response? Are we walking in fellowship with him, or hiding in the darkness? Have we received the new life that Christ offers as a free gift, or are we still trying to work things out in our own strength? Is God a living reality in our lives, or just the distant glimmer of a bygone age? The answers to some of these questions may determine not just how we spend the rest of our lives, but where we spend eternity.

Questions to Consider:

(i)   Which of Jesus' commandments challenges us the most in Matthew 5.21-48? How did Jesus live out these principles in his personal life, and how can his example help us?

(ii)   Read chapters 7 and 8 of Romans. What is the main ingredient in chapter 8 that is missing in chapter 7? Why does adhering to an external set of rules cause so many problems in the first of these two chapters, and why are they no longer a concern for Paul afterwards?

(iii)   Compare 1 Kings 18.21, Ephesians 4.14 and James 1.5-8,17. Are we wavering in our Christian walk, or trying to compromise between two lifestyles at the same time? What might encourage us to live more wholeheartedly for Christ? Are there any unsurrendered parts of our lives that need to be brought under the Lordship of Christ?

---

14 BABYLON IN THE CHURCH

If, as we have seen, there is a conflict that takes place in our hearts on a daily basis, there is also a battle being waged by the powers of darkness against the church as a whole, a war that has continued unabated for the last two thousand years.

Jesus promised that, on the solid foundation of Peter's confession of him as Messiah, 'I will build my church, and the gates of Hades will not overcome it' (Matt. 16.18). However, just as the children of Israel through their own disobedience reaped part of the curse that Balaam had been unable to inflict from outside (Num. 25.1-3), so today parts of the church seem literally hell-bent on sabotaging themselves from within.

Satan is an intruder. He masquerades as an angel of light. He so easily slips into our church gatherings without us noticing. He is skilled at blending in and is constantly looking for chinks in our armour. The American preacher Vance Havner once reminded us that, 'The devil is not persecuting Christianity nowadays - he is professing it. He is not fighting churches - he is joining them'.[1]

Jesus told a parable about a field of wheat to which an enemy came during the night and sowed darnel (Matt. 13.24-30 NET). Darnel, though poisonous, looks indistinguishable from wheat while it is growing. It is only when the ears sprout at harvest time that the difference becomes obvious: the darnel continues to stand rigidly upright, while the heads of grain on the wheat cause it to bow down.

Like the darnel, Babylon is unbroken and unbowed. It subtly creeps into the church by stealth and attempts to strangle the life out of the wheat, that which is truly yielded to God. Left unchecked, this process can leave the church indistinguishable from the world around it, and effectively neutered. We need to be on our guard to spot its entry and stop its onward march.

There are three main windows through which the spirit of Babylon seeks to infiltrate, and all have been open at different stages in history. These correspond in large degree to three different levels of the church's structure: the local congregation, an entire denomination, and the church at national level. We will now consider the nature of each of these threats in turn, and how they can all end up infecting the body of Christ, from cells right up to entire limbs and organs.

1. The Lure of Self-Advancement

Jesus came to bring relationship, not another religion. However, as we saw in the last chapter, Paul warns how man-centred religious thought, based on outward display and exaltation of self, can hijack authentic faith. Such religion, though couched as a pursuit of the things of God, is in reality a vehicle for pride and self-righteousness. As an example, Paul talks of how he was 'advancing in Judaism beyond many of my own age among my people and was extremely zealous for the traditions of my fathers' (Gal. 1.14). So easily today the church can fall prey to these false ways of thinking and become indistinguishable from other religious systems.

It is not difficult to see how easily this self-centred ladder of progression can take hold in our own spiritual life. Just when we are beginning to get things right in our lives and to make headway in our battle against sin, we are often in the greatest danger. So effortlessly we can turn from the tax collector into the Pharisee. Man-centred religion is the natural default of the fallen human condition. It is too easy to forget that our righteous deeds are no more than filthy rags in God's sight (Is. 64.6).

These delusions of grandeur can cause us to get puffed up by a sense of our own importance relative to everyone else. A similar situation arose in the gospels, when James and John came up and *told* Jesus, 'we want you to do for us whatever we ask' (always a bad start when approaching the king of the universe)! They then ask to be given special places at his right and left hand in heaven, which, not surprisingly, did not win them many accolades from the other disciples (Mark 10.35-41).

This same root of pride often manifests itself in our churches in a performance mentality. And it is not just preachers or worship leaders who can get sucked into this: we can all get caught out. Jesus warns those who announce their acts of piety and giving 'with trumpets' that they have already 'received their reward in full' (Matt. 6.2). He says the same of those who 'love to pray standing in the synagogues and on the street corners to be seen by others' (6.5). And he berates the Pharisees in no uncertain terms for such elaborate displays:

'Everything they do is done for people to see: they make their phylacteries wide and the tassels on their garments long; they love the place of honour at banquets and the most important seats in the synagogues; they love to be greeted with respect in the market-places and to be called "Rabbi" by others.

(Matt. 23.5-7)

A variant on this is the sin of presumptuousness. There are many examples of this to learn from in scripture. We can see this in the 'I-can-do-this-better' Messiah complex displayed by Elihu in the Book of Job, who, describing himself as 'one who has perfect knowledge' presumes to speak 'on God's behalf' (Job 36.2-4). We can see it in the early life of Moses who takes it upon himself to kill an Egyptian who is abusing his authority, and then attempts to interfere in an argument between two Hebrew slaves that has nothing to do with him (Ex. 2.11-14). We see it in Paul's warning against 'busybodies' who have so much time on their hands that they devote it to trying to run everyone else's lives (2 Thess. 3.11; 1 Tim. 5.13).

A still greater threat is the menace of factionalism. Paul castigates the church in Corinth because 'one of you says, "I follow Paul"; another, "I follow Apollos"; another, "I follow Cephas"; still another, "I follow Christ" ' (1 Cor. 1.12). He warns the Ephesian elders that 'even from your own number men will arise and distort the truth in order to draw away disciples after them' (Acts 20.30). It easy to see from Absalom's rebellion against David how competing power-bases can so quickly lead to a disastrous split.

Pride does not just manifest in assertive ways, however, but in defensive ways as well. One mindset from the world that so often creeps into our churches today is an 'entitlement mentality' where we become overly preoccupied with our rights, or a 'victim mentality' where we feel we are being denied them. Such a manner of thinking rose up in the early church when Jews of a Greek cultural background felt that their widows were being overlooked in the daily distribution of food (Acts 6.1). It is all too easy to forget that Jesus *'did not demand and cling to his rights as God*, but laid aside his mighty power and glory, taking the disguise of a slave and becoming like men' (Phil 2.6-7, *Living Bible*). By contrast, a demanding spirit is never satisfied: 'The leech has two daughters. "Give! Give!" they cry.' (Prov. 30.15).

Such pride also far too often appears as a spirit of defensiveness or stubbornness. This can arise individually when a particular church member needs a gentle rebuke, or collectively when a (perhaps new) pastor tries to introduce change within a church, or to equip it with fresh vision. Such resistance to the work of God has many precedents in scripture and it again reflects a man-centred Babylon mentality.

There are, for example, the controlling spirits who fear their power base will be eroded (compare Athaliah in 2 Chronicles 22.10); there are the 'can't-do-it' conservatives who resist every challenge (the ten spies in Numbers 13.31-33); there are the intransigents who secretly plot obstacles to any advance of God's work (Sanballat, Tobias and Geshem in Nehemiah 6.1-19); there are the self-proclaimed 'whistleblowers' who record a catalogue of perceived misdeeds (the spies who infiltrate the Gentile church in Galatians 2.4); there are the unsubmissive souls who stand up and fight against leadership head on (Korah, Dathan and Abiram in Numbers 16.1-34); and there are grumblers and malcontents lurking in the background, ready to wield the knife at the opportune time (Judas Iscariot in John 12.4-6).

On top of all this there is a whole litany of other problems that pastors often need to contend with, such as gossip, backbiting, personality clashes, self-righteousness, classism, sexism, racism, ageism, and so on. The list seems to be endless. As the church prepares for a great end-time harvest of souls, these may become significant issues that will have to be addressed in the future as many unchurched seekers and raw new believers come into the church.

The difficulty for us is that it always seems deceptively easy to identify such problems in those around us, while being completely blind to their presence in ourselves. It is always far too simple for us to point fingers and cast stones at others, when in fact God is putting each one of *us* under the spotlight. 'Being certain that we are right' can be a big problem for everyone in the church today. Sometimes it takes many decades of being moulded, humbled and broken for this mindset to change.

For example, it took a lifetime for God to soften and bend the spirit of Jacob, the father of the twelve tribes of Israel. He starts off by pressuring his brother to sell him his birthright, and then tricks his father into giving him his brother's rightful blessing as well (Gen. 25.33; 27.18-29). Later he tries to strike a '*quid pro quo*' bargain with God, whereby he will serve God in exchange for continued blessings (28.20-22). It is finally as God confronts and injures him at the ford of Jabbok, when he is fearful about having to meet his long-lost brother Esau, that his heart begins to give way: yet even then he is still making demands (32.24-30). Only later does a real brokenness of spirit become manifest, when God unexpectedly restores back what has previously been taken away (Gen. 37.34-35; 48.11).

Likewise, Paul started out life as an 'angry young man', viciously persecuting the church (Acts 8.3). As with Jacob's dramatic encounter with God at Jabbok, the shock of being confronted and blinded by Jesus on the road to Damascus radically changes the course of his life (9.1-19). But even in an early letter like Galatians, we might still discern rough edges to his character: he still seems a little dismissive of those in authority, and publically confronts Peter at Antioch, just as he later falls out with Barnabas (Gal. 2.6; 2.11-14; Acts 15.37-40).[2] If we compare his final letter, however, a very different Paul emerges, humbled, softened, and ready now to face death (2 Tim. 4.6-18).

So often the Christian life begins with pride, immaturity and lack of brokenness before the Lord. Qualities like loyalty, faithfulness, longsuffering and submissiveness take a lifetime to be fully worked out. Such a journey involves many setbacks and misfortunes and a lot of honesty and heart-searching before God, as well as a patience and generosity of spirit towards the failings of others.

It is by constantly rubbing against each other that the rough, jagged edges of the stones that form the beds of many mountain streams gradually become smooth and rounded. Let us, therefore, submit ourselves to God's gentle process of erosion, that each one of us may lose our sharp edges and be shaped more into the likeness of Christ.

2. The Lure of Secularism

If we need a Christ-like view of each other, we also need it in ever-greater measure towards the culture around us. We live in a kaleidoscopically shifting world. Public opinion concerning many key moral issues has moved significantly over the last fifty years. Should we as the church try and keep in step with this culture shift, or should we be willing to stand firm, and endure howls of disapproval from politicians, the press and the wider media?

The dilemma is certainly not a new one. Ever since its inception the church has struggled to maintain Biblical truth in the face of an intoxicating web of worldly ideas. For centuries it tried to accommodate Greek philosophical models which pictured a remote and inscrutable God who could only relate to the world through a chain of intermediate beings linked by steadily decreasing rungs of divinity.[3] The results of this compromise degenerated inevitably into the veneration of angels, saints, icons and other holy objects, alongside profound attacks on the nature of the Trinity.

Today we seem no better in defending ourselves from the rationalistic worldview of the secular culture around us. Since the Enlightenment we have been rushing ahead at breakneck speed to jettison the supernatural and miraculous and to enthrone human reason in their place. A classic symptom of this can be seen in a statement by the influential German theologian Rudolf Bultmann:

> Man's knowledge and mastery of the world have advanced to such an extent through science and technology that it is no longer possible for anyone seriously to hold to the New Testament view of the world.[4]

In 1900 the 'Sunday World' magazine asked a variety of influential figures the question, 'What is the chief danger that confronts us in the new century?' The response of William Booth, the founder of the Salvation Army, was 'religion without the Holy Ghost, Christianity without Christ, forgiveness without repentance, salvation without regeneration, politics without God, heaven without hell.'[5] (His reply stood in stark contrast to the then Archbishop of Canterbury, Frederick Temple, whose only response was that he had 'not the slightest idea', the kind of vacuous equivocation which all too often afflicts our established church).

Booth's prediction has proved more than justified, and is being fulfilled even more rapidly in the century we now live in. Much of the Bible has either been thrown out of the window, or consigned to the realm of mythology, with God being demoted to a benign 'Santa Claus' figure who seems little concerned with sin or judgement.

Perhaps the climax of this headlong capitulation to liberal values has been across the Atlantic, where the so-called 'Jesus Seminar' sets itself up in the place of God by pronouncing 'authoritative' judgements on the accuracy and reliability of Jesus' words in the gospels, forgetting, of course, that in the end God's word will judge *them*, and not vice versa!

All this effectively renders the gospel worthless and offers no hope to the broken world around us. It is small wonder that, as broadcaster Jeremy Paxman pointedly observes, more people now belong to the Royal Society for the Protection of Birds than attend church regularly in the United Kingdom.[6]

This wholescale slide into relativism has led to a growing tendency within the church to rubber-stamp every passing trend in society. Paul's prediction about end-time culture 'having a form of godliness but denying its power' (2 Tim. 3.5) could not be more relevant today.

In the Old Testament God remonstrates with priests who 'do not distinguish between the holy and the common' and 'teach that there is no difference between the unclean and the clean' (Ezek. 22.26) and prophets who 'whitewash these deeds for them by false visions and lying divinations' (v. 28). His warning to them, as to the entire nation, is that 'I will pour out my wrath on them and consume them with my fiery anger, bringing down on their own heads all they have done' (v. 31). It is a warning that we should urgently heed today.

The corrosive effect of this culture drift within the church can happen quite unconsciously in our own lives. We are often unaware, for example, of the slow drip-feed that secular television has on our thinking, subtly promoting a Babylonian worldview. In a way it functions exactly like the telescreen in George Orwell's *Nineteen Eighty-Four*, where viewers are blissfully ignorant of the fact that they are slowly being brainwashed.

This is particularly the case in the news agenda, for example, which creates a synthetic reality that so easily convinces us that the world is run solely by the laws of politics, economics and human psychology, irrespective of what God is doing. We can be easily coaxed into thinking that everything is decided in Westminster, Brussels or Washington, and to forget the influence wielded by powerful spiritual forces behind the scenes. We can easily take on non-Biblical views about gender or morality which are being extensively purveyed without realising that our minds are being subtly programmed.

Very quickly this can begin to influence our perception of truth. We have seen how in Babylon right and wrong is laid out on a spectrum. But in the spiritual realm there are no shades of grey. We cannot serve two masters. We are either under God's rule or Satan's rule.

The same trap we face in imbibing aspects of a secular worldview can also tempt us to draw in elements from other religions on a 'pick-and-mix' basis. There is of course a legitimate place for constructive dialogue with other faith groups, and even for working together towards common objectives such as social justice, abortion law reform, or protecting the rights of religious minorities. What plunges us into the realm of apostasy, however, is joining together to worship different gods, or even worshipping the same God in two profoundly incompatible ways (the golden calf in the wilderness was, after all, intended in Exodus 32.5 as an alternative *representation* of Yahweh). This crosses over a red line which we are repeatedly warned in scripture not to approach.

As an example of this, a multi-faith service in Newcastle Cathedral in May 1984 included an incarnation of the Hindu god Vishnu repeatedly acclaimed as 'Lord Rama, King Rama, Lord of All, King Rama, Lord Rama', followed later by more chanting, dancing and the offering of flowers as another Hindu effigy was brought into the cathedral. Alongside this the Qur'an was read, with Sikh and Baha'i contributions added to the mix. The only mention of Jesus during the entire service was an oblique reference in the last line of the final hymn.[7]

Not only do such events turn the church into a kind of 'bargain basement' religious supermarket, but they profoundly misrepresent the God of the Bible and the nature of the incarnation. When multi-faith worship takes place in the temple in Jerusalem in Ezekiel 8.7-16, a terrifying judgement is unleashed in Jerusalem in the following chapter. And the same warning against such overt syncretism appears again in Zephaniah:

> 'I will stretch out my hand against Judah
>   and against all who live in Jerusalem.
> I will destroy every remnant of Baal worship in this place,
>   the very names of the idolatrous priests –
> those who bow down on the roofs
>   to worship the starry host,
> *those who bow down and swear by the LORD*
>   *and who also swear by Molek ....*' (Zeph. 1.4-5)

However well-intentioned such interfaith initiatives are, therefore, they take the church into a profoundly dangerous area. As with the heated issue of gender and sexuality, what matters in the end is what God thinks, not how we think he ought to think.

A further area in which the church seems all too eager to follow the ways of the world is in the realm of money. Paul writes that:

> Those who want to get rich fall into temptation and a trap and into many foolish and harmful desires that plunge people into ruin and destruction. For the love of money is a root of all kinds of evil. Some people, eager for money, have wandered from the faith and pierced themselves with many griefs.
>
> (1 Tim. 6.9-10)

In our dealings with money we can so easily take exactly the same attitude as the society around us. The Irish poet John Boyle O'Reilly (1844-1890) once mocked the church's attitudes to finance in the following words:

> The organised charity, scrimped and iced
> In the name of a cautious, statistical Christ.[8]

Human arithmetic often works against God's purposes because it *limits* God. Too often we forget that God's mathematics is completely different from ours. The scope of God's resources goes far beyond anything we could ever imagine, and yet too often we squeeze him into a tightly-fitting box.

At the same time, material affluence can also be a huge threat to discipleship because of the complacency it generates (Deut. 6.10-12). The pursuit of prosperity can become a god in its own right. Jesus condemned the Pharisees' attitude to money as 'an abomination in the sight of God' (Luke 16.15 ESV). Likewise, he warns the church in Laodicea,

You say, "I am rich; I have acquired wealth and do not need a thing." But you do not realise that you are wretched, pitiful, poor, blind and naked. I counsel you to buy from me gold refined in the fire, so that you can become rich; and white clothes to wear, so that you can cover your shameful nakedness; and salve to put on your eyes, so that you can see. (Rev. 3.17-18)

Where cathedrals once demonstrated the glory of God, they are now, like St Paul's, often overshadowed by vast edifices celebrating the glory of Mammon. We need to be very careful that the same thing does not happen in our own lives or in our churches. Jacob only had the major encounter with God that we discussed earlier *after* he had let go of all his possessions (Gen. 32.22-24). Likewise, Jesus calls us to a radically different attitude towards material things, warning that 'those of you who do not give up everything you have *cannot* be my disciples' (Luke 14.33).

In all these respects the church can too easily become a magnet lining up with the world's way of thinking. We run indiscriminately after every passing fad and fashion, failing to discern, unlike the company of prophets in the Elisha's day, that there is 'death in the pot' (2 Kings 4.40). As a result, the message we offer becomes cheapened and corrupted. We are called to offer the world living water, not to provide drinks from a contaminated spring.

As a result, there is a tightrope we have to walk where we need to remain relevant to the culture around us without losing our distinctiveness. It is all too easy to dilute the gospel and capitulate to the false gods of personality, entertainment, or New Age principles in order to court popularity. True revival, however, will only come when we humble ourselves before God and wholeheartedly seek his will for our land. Anything short of this will consign millions of souls needlessly to a lost eternity.

3. The Lure of State Power

The third way in which Babylon seeks to wrest control of the church is through a wholescale takeover at the top. This is what took place after the conversion of Constantine in the 4th century AD. Within a very short space of time the church was transformed from an illegal underground into a privileged elite, holding all the levers of state power.

In many ways it was the kiss of death. Firstly, it gave rulers an unprecedented right to interfere with the internal affairs of the church. This took church doctrine into the realm of politics, where it was no longer a matter of prayerful reflection but of backstage manoeuvring and intrigue, based on which emperor happened to be in power at the time. During the 4th century a succession of emperors of different theological persuasions kept tampering with the Nicene Creed, the church's major summary of doctrine. As the pendulum swung backwards and forwards, leading bishops could be relieved of their posts and even sent into exile. Athanasius, for example, who held to an orthodox Biblical view of the deity of Christ, was dismissed from his position no less than five times.

Secondly, the church under official patronage shifted within a very short time from being a heavily persecuted minority, where thousands had been crucified, to a position of new-found respectability. Whereas previously making a stand for Christ might have cost someone their life, joining the church now became a socially advantageous move, shifting a life-or-death decision to a mere lifestyle choice. Many simply continued their previous life under the cosmetic veneer of conforming to the new social norms, practising their old religion behind closed doors.

This tendency inevitably brought with it a host of alien cultural practices into the church. In crude terms, the church morphed over time into the very things it had tried to replace: pagan buildings were turned into church buildings, the pantheon of gods became the communion of saints, the cults of Venus and Aphrodite drifted into the veneration of Mary, and idolatrous festivals were 'Christianised'. Even the title 'pontifex maximus' (supreme pontiff), originally used by the pagan high priest in Rome, and later adopted by the emperors themselves, was subsequently taken up as an unofficial title by the papacy.

As a result, the nature of worship began to change. Justo and Catherine González write that

> The ritual of Christian worship began to imitate the formalities of the imperial court, with all their distinctions between various levels in the civil hierarchy. Christ was depicted as sitting on a heavenly throne, in a posture which resembles that of the emperors on their thrones. Even the cross was often studied with precious gems. Anything to obscure the fact that the One whom the church worshipped was a poor carpenter from Galilee, who had been condemned to death as an outlaw by Roman authorities.[9]

With new and powerful beneficiaries, huge amounts of wealth had begun pouring into the church. At first much of this was used in benefiting society, being channelled into building schools and hospitals and relieving the poor. Increasingly, however, money was siphoned off to individuals at the upper echelons of the church. By the Middle Ages many popes were living lives of debauchery, intrigue and extravagance no less corrupt than any Roman emperor before them.

Before the dawn of the Reformation the church was being run like a major financial corporation: it collected ten per cent of everyone's income but paid no taxes, and effectively operated a 'pay-as-you-pray' policy, whereby anything that could be sold was sold: relics, church posts, indulgences (which offered a kind of 'get-out-of-jail free card' in purgatory). On top of this christenings, marriages and funerals or any kind of priestly intercession incurred extra charges, which fell heavily on the poorest in society.

The most serious charge, however, is that the church changed from being the victim to being the bully. Within just a century of the most extreme persecution under Diocletian, Christianity switched from being *illegal* for anybody to being *imposed* on everybody. This heavy-handedness became particularly evident in the church's treatment of the Jews. I spell this out this extensively in my book *The Forgotten Bride*, but will summarise the main points here.

It began with the imperially sanctioned Council of Nicaea in AD 325, which took the decision to separate Easter from the celebration of the Jewish Passover, and forbade Christians to celebrate Passover with Jews, or to engage in formal worship on the Jewish Sabbath. Ratifying the decree, Constantine went on record as saying: 'Let us then have nothing in common with the detestable Jewish crowd ... and withdraw ourselves from all participation in their baseness.'[10]

From AD 329 onwards, punitive sanctions were placed on those converting to Judaism. A further edict in 353 allowed for a convert's property to be confiscated and taken over by the state. By 409, a Jew attempting to convert a Christian could be held guilty of High Treason.

Other restrictions against the Jews started becoming enshrined in imperial law. In 438 all Jews were excluded from public service and forbidden to build new places of worship. In 553 Justinian forbade the reading of the Mishnah and restricted what could be taught in synagogues. He also attempted to close down all synagogues in North Africa, and converted some into churches. In 614 the emperor Heraclius outlawed Judaism completely in the Byzantine Empire and many Jews were compelled to convert.

Alongside this a flood of oppressive restrictions was brought in by local church councils and synods. In 653 AD the Eighth Council of Toledo banned circumcision and required Jewish converts to Christianity to stone or burn to death those of their number who relapsed. The following year the Visigothic rulers in Spain, aided and abetted by the church, made it illegal for Jews to observe Passover or other Feasts, keep the Sabbath or observe Jewish dietary laws. By 694 the Fourteenth Council of Toledo had required all Jews to be sold into slavery, with their property confiscated, and all Jewish children over the age of seven to be forcibly removed and educated in monasteries.

When we add to this litany of persecution the unspeakable atrocities of the Crusades, the state-sponsored torture of the Spanish Inquisition, and the fact that anyone opposing the church could be burnt at the stake, we are left with a horrifying legacy. It is small wonder that the Protestant Reformers identified end-time Babylon in Revelation with the might of the Catholic Church.[11]

However, Protestant attempts at theocracy, such as the short-lived takeover of Münster by the Anabaptists in 1534, where polygamy and compulsory baptism were introduced, do not inspire much confidence either. Nor, in all its legalistic rectitude, does the Puritan takeover of England, with its ban on Christmas, the Sabbath rigidly enforced, people encouraged to dress in black, and neighbours exhorted to spy on each other (all in complete disregard of Colossians 2.16-17). In particular Cromwell's brutal treatment of the Irish, massacring the towns of Wexford and Drogheda, and sending many Irish children to the West Indies to work the sugar plantations as slave labourers, reflects some of the same antichrist spirit as the worst excesses of the corrupted Catholicism he was trying to destroy.

Even the milder forms of church establishment adopted across much of Protestant northern Europe have proved to be ultimately self-destructive. Far from buttressing the spiritual life of a nation, they simply dilute it. State-sponsored churches end up far too often rubber-stamping the actions of godless governments and generating a culture of nominalism and complacency within their ranks, without any encouragement to make a personal commitment to Christ. In Denmark, for instance, 75% of the population are registered members of the national church but less than 20% consider religion an important part of their lives, and only 3% regularly attend Sunday services.[12]

The same is true, to a lesser degree, in the Church of England. Too often it has been paralysed by the deadening hold of tradition, the numbing wind of compromise, and the stifling desire to mean all things to all men. Britain is the only country in the world (apart from Iran) to have guaranteed seats for clerics in its Parliament, and yet the only impact has been to neuter the church by tying it to the institutions of state, preventing it from giving a clear message on the key moral issues of our time. Despite its many remarkable successes, the Anglican church has all too often lost itself in a morass of contradictions, plunging it down to the lowest common denominator of agreement.[13]

Elsewhere the love affair between church and state has produced results that are far more insidious, giving rise to a lethal cocktail of unquestioning faith and unbridled patriotism. When we consider what Hitler was able to achieve, with the full support of two-thirds of the German church, we can see the huge capacity for evil to prevail. Nothing damages the church more quickly than to become the passive cheerleader for the actions of a cruel and godless regime, bestowing a Christian halo of approval on what is the manifest work of Satan.

A particularly chilling example of such state control of the church today can be seen in the Three-Self churches in China. Despite a façade of independence, they are ruled with an iron fist by the Communist Party, which can dictate how many people can be baptized per year and what material is allowed in preaching. While Beijing encourages certain subjects (such as patriotism or social responsibility) to be expounded upon widely, other topics (such as the resurrection of Christ or his second coming) are specifically outlawed. In many churches representations of the cross or scripture verses have been replaced by pictures of President Xi and Communist Party propaganda, and CCTV monitoring of congregations is now commonplace.

The Chinese state church offers just a small picture of what an end-time church might look like in the West, with a doctored Bible, emasculated clergy and severe government restrictions.

While we are still some way from this point, we have already drawn attention in Chapter Ten to the forces at work in society that would like to restrict what is taught in churches and to shut down anything deemed as 'extremism' or 'hate speech'. In Revelation 11.7-8 the beast who wages war on the divinely-appointed witnesses of God is associated with the name 'Sodom'. We need to be ready for a time when we either choose to belong to a neutralised state-sanctioned church, or throw our lot in with underground Christians and risk the full force of the law against us.

Jesus left us in no doubt as to how the future might unfold:

> 'Then you will be handed over to be persecuted and put to death, and you will be hated by all nations because of me. At that time many will turn away from the faith and will betray and hate each other, and many false prophets will appear and deceive many people. Because of the increase of wickedness, the love of most will grow cold, but the one who stands firm to the end will be saved. And this gospel of the kingdom will be preached in the whole world as a testimony to all nations, and then the end will come.' (Matt. 24.9-14)

It is for the sake of this gospel that, despite everything thrown against it, the church needs above all to be able to stand firm and fight for what it believes. Now is not the time to capitulate to the forces of darkness.

Above all we need constantly to remember our persecuted brothers and sisters around the world who are already going through these trials, and to intercede daily on their behalf. One day it could be our turn for a loud knocking at the door.

Questions to Consider:

(i) 'Do nothing from selfishness or conceit, but in humility count others better than yourselves' (Phil 2.3). How seriously do we take this verse? How could it impact our relationships with Christians from very different social, racial or intellectual backgrounds, or with different theological standpoints? To what extent should it also apply to our relationships with non-Christians?

(ii) Read the parable of the wise and foolish virgins (Matt.25.1-13). What happened to those who were not prepared? What does it mean to 'buy' oil? (Compare Rev. 3.18). If Jesus came back tonight, would we be ready, or have we become distracted by other things (as described in Luke 21.34-36)?

(iii) What ungodly forces of control can we see at work in the church? Do they manifest in our own lives or in the way we treat others?

15 BABYLON TRANSFORMED?

Western Europe today is closer to the interplay of forces that shaped first century Israel than at any time in its history. Then, as now, there was a clash between religious Babylon (then, the Jewish religious elite but today, over much of the continent, the forces of Islam) and the secular, godless Babylon of the ruling authorities. Outwardly these two tectonic forces seem to be polar opposites, but actually both are distant cousins in that they major on what man can achieve by his own efforts, as opposed to what God has done for us in Christ. Both, in a sense, are attempting to build towers to heaven.

Now, as then, true Christianity is caught in the middle, locked between the twin extremes of religious fanaticism on the one hand and secular indifference on the other. More and more, it finds itself vilified by both sides and fighting for its very existence. To the secularist, evangelical Christianity is tarred with the same brush of fanaticism and intolerance as radical Islam. To the Islamist, Christianity is corrupted by the same liberalism and moral relativism as the decaying world around it.

If today, as in Acts, the secular side still appears slightly more accommodating and reasonable, it is because it displays traces of the 'common grace' to which we referred in Chapter Eleven (even if that reservoir of tolerance towards Christians seems to be steadily diminishing). Our educated secular civilisation, despite its rebellion against Biblical values, still carries traces of godly principles remaining from the impact of centuries of Christian heritage, which narrow religion often obliterates because it marks a fundamental denial of God's true character.

I believe, however, that it is secular civilisation with its increasingly mesmerising, seductive influence that ultimately poses by far the greatest danger to today's church. Behind a benign exterior, sinister forces are operating, like a wolf in sheep's clothing. While there are many good things we can still admire in Babylon from an earthly point of view, the spiritual forces pulling her strings are utterly corrupt, as Revelation makes clear.

As Christians, we face the same dilemmas today in responding to these pressures that our forebears of the first century faced. Broadly speaking, we are faced with three clear options:

1. Withdrawal

The simplest choice is to do what the disciples did immediately after the crucifixion and to retreat behind closed doors. Many have tried that option in the past, whether it be the Jews who concealed themselves in closed communities such as Qumran, Christians who hid in monasteries to protect themselves from the ravages of the outside world, or more recent groups such as the Exclusive Brethren who have attempted to hive themselves off from the rest of humanity.

Although for a small minority undergoing intense persecution, hiding may be the only realistic option to stay alive, for the vast majority of us God is not calling us to live like hermits. It is the kings of the earth who will hide when God's judgement comes (Rev. 6.15-17). Jesus warns us about what happened to the servant who hid his talent instead of trading with it (Matt. 25.24-30).

Nor is it healthy to raise ourselves up to some kind of ethereal higher plane, disconnected from the rest of the world, like Simeon Stylites (c. 390-459), who spent 37 years on the top of a pillar. We are not called to look down on our world but to step into the midst of it.

God's creation mandate to us was to fill the earth and subdue it. Babel was an attempt to contravene that by gathering everyone together in one place. Yet so often this is precisely what we do in our churches today! It is striking that the Jerusalem church in Acts, having received the first full-scale antidote to Babel at Pentecost, ends up suffering the same fate as that original stricken city - to be scattered in every direction (Acts 8.1). And yet, ironically, this was what really lit the touchpaper for the exponential growth of the body of Christ (8.4). Jesus' updating of the original 'be fruitful' creation mandate, sending us to '*go* and make disciples of all nations' (Matt. 28.19) means precisely what it says: it is not an invitation to bury our talents or hide our lamps.

Today it is still very tempting to isolate ourselves into 'holy huddles' to avoid being contaminated by the world. However, despite the comfort that can come from such a cult-like withdrawal, it can so easily degenerate into paranoia and a doomsday mentality where we begin to focus inwards rather than outwards. As a result, we can all too easily get sucked in by conspiracy theories which paint a dystopian picture of secret cabals trying to take over the world, forgetting that any such events need to conform to God's own agenda and timing. Many of these were conspiracy theories originally rooted in libellous claims about the Jews, but have now fanned out in all manner of directions.

There is nothing new about such 'fake news': Paul warns about it in his second letter to the Thessalonians, where he warns them, 'not to be quickly shaken in mind or excited, either by spirit or by word, or *by letter purporting to be from us*, to the effect that the day of the Lord has come' (2.2 RSV). As Christians we seem to be particularly susceptible to uncritically accepting such wildly unsubstantiated claims, judging from the number of fake gospels that went into circulation in the early centuries of the church. The warning of James that 'a great forest is set on fire by a small spark' (3.5) could not be more appropriate in today's world where one tall story spawns a thousand retweets.

Scripture gives us very clear tests for any piece of so-called 'information': to investigate it thoroughly at source (Ezra 5.17; Luke 1.3-4), to corroborate it through *independent* witnesses (Matt. 18.16; 2 Cor. 13.1) and to weigh it (Prov. 18.17; 1 Thess. 5.21-22). In an age that jumps on every bandwagon concerned with UFOs, the Vatican, the CIA, the 'deep state', and so on, we need to exercise extreme caution. The Bible is emphatic:

'Do not call conspiracy
  everything this people calls a conspiracy;
do not fear what they fear,

and do not dread it.
The LORD Almighty is the one you are to regard as holy,
  he is the one you are to fear,
  he is the one you are to dread. (Is. 8.12-13)

Such preoccupations can end up as being distractions from the vital work of spreading the gospel, praying in God's kingdom and serving others. Paul warns of a time when 'itching ears' will 'turn aside to myths'. His advice to Timothy (and by extension to us) to counter this is to 'keep your head in all situations, endure hardship, do the work of an evangelist, discharge all the duties of your ministry' (2 Tim. 4.3-5).

As Christians, then, we are not called to be hiding away in theological bunkers, waiting for an apocalypse that never arrives (Jonah 4.5) or desperately trying to avoid being contaminated by the world around us (Luke 10.30-32). On the contrary, Jesus is calling us to look outwards, to live boldly and to seek to impact the world, rather than escape from it. We can live out every day as if it were our last, without tying ourselves into knots about when the end will happen (Matt. 24.36). Ecclesiastes warns that 'whoever watches the wind will not plant; whoever looks at the clouds will not reap' (11.4).

Nor is there any purpose in trying to run away from situations, like Jonah, instead of co-operating with God to transform them. Jesus warns that 'No one who puts his hand to the plough and looks back is fit for the kingdom of God' (Luke 9.62 ESV). The nation to which Jonah had been sent had a reputation for extreme brutality and godlessness. Yet despite Jonah's reluctance to get involved, God's purposes prevailed, causing 120,000 people to be saved.

In the same way, Jesus is not pulling us *out* of the front line, but rather sending us back *into* it:

'My prayer is not that you take them out of the world but that you protect them from the evil one. ... As you sent me into the world, I have sent them into the world' (John 17.15,18).

Rather than concealing ourselves, therefore, our calling is to live as salt and light in the midst of a broken and hurting world:

'You are the salt of the earth. But if the salt loses its saltiness, how can it be made salty again? It is no longer good for anything, except to be thrown out and trampled underfoot.

'You are the light of the world. A town built on a hill cannot be hidden. Neither do people light a lamp and put it under a bowl. Instead they put it on its stand, and it gives light to everyone in the house. In the same way, let your light shine before others, that they may see your good deeds and glorify your Father in heaven. (Matt. 5.13-16)

In all things, therefore, we are called to be agents of transformation, bringing a blessing wherever we go. Running or hiding is not an option. As lights in the world, we are commanded to follow in the footsteps of Jesus.

2. Accommodation

Another option in the wake of the pressures around us is to 'go with the flow' and to try and compromise with the world. This is an insidious snare. As we saw in the last chapter, the spirit of Babylon acts like a virus, seeking to infiltrate God's people. Like Lot we may become hesitant and double-minded, reluctant to escape from the world's comforting allure and at risk of being absorbed by the culture around us.

Over and over again in the Old Testament Israel fell into this trap. In the wilderness they were tempted to build a golden calf, and 3,000 died as a result (Ex. 32.1-28). At Ai Israel were defeated because Achan was tempted by a coat from Babylon (Josh. 7.2-12; 21). At Shittim, as mentioned in the last chapter, the Israelites brought a curse on themselves through unfaithfulness that Balaam had been unable to bring about through divination (Num. 25.1-3).

The lure of surrounding nations was a constant stumbling-block. Moses was warned by God in the wilderness 'not to make a treaty with those who live in the land where you are going, or they will be a snare among you' (Ex. 34.12). Israel was continually compromised by its desire to resemble other nations (1 Sam. 8.19-20). We hear in the book of Ezra of the problems caused by intermarriage with pagans, with the inevitable temptation towards idolatry that this produces (Ezra 9.1-4), a situation that also arose under Nehemiah (Neh. 13.23-29).

Similar problems surface in the New Testament. Seduced by the lure of secret wealth, combined with wanting to *look good* in the eyes of the church, Ananias and Sapphira make a tragic mistake in dishonesty. They were not being *compelled* to sell their field but just wanted respect and admiration (Acts 5.1-10). Likewise Simon the Sorcerer thought he could buy the gift of laying on of hands with money (Acts 8.18-19).

Jesus reminds us that the broad road that leads to destruction (Matt. 7.13), yet so often we hunt for the easy way out. The invitation to cut corners was the essence of one of Satan's temptations of Jesus in the wilderness, which offered the glittering (but ultimately illusory) prospect of achieving earthly dominion while avoiding the cross. This explains the vehemence of Jesus' response to Peter when he tried to suggest the same strategy, as we saw at the beginning of Chapter Thirteen. And yet many Christians today are still tempted by a crossless Christianity, which seems to offer a priority lane through to health, wealth and happiness.

Such short cuts will not give us the victory in the battles we face in our lives. In fact, they may represent a capitulation, since it is the *unsurrendered* parts of our lives that are slowly destroying us. Jesus made it very clear that we need to be ready to give up *everything* if we are truly to be his disciples, and if we truly want to gain the upper hand against the powers of darkness:

> 'Suppose one of you wants to build a tower. Won't you first sit down and estimate the cost to see if you have enough money to complete it? For if you lay the foundation and are not able to finish it, everyone who sees it will ridicule you, saying, "This person began to build and wasn't able to finish."
>
> 'Or suppose a king is about to go to war against another king. Won't he first sit down and consider whether he is able with ten thousand men to oppose the one coming against him with twenty thousand? If he is not able, he will send a delegation while the other is still a long way off and will ask for terms of peace. **In the same way, those of you who do not give up everything you have cannot be my disciples.**'
>
> (Luke 14.28-33)

Paul warns us 'do *not* conform to the pattern of this world, but be transformed by the renewing of your mind' (Rom. 12.2). In the face of the pluralistic society around us, he tells us not to be 'yoked together with unbelievers' (2 Cor. 6.14).

John likewise warns us in his first letter:

> Do not love the world or anything in the world. If anyone loves the world, love for the Father is not in them. For everything in the world – the lust of the flesh, the lust of the eyes, and the pride of life – comes not from the Father but from the world. The world and its desires pass away, but whoever does the will of God lives for ever. (1 John 2.15-17)

Going beyond this, Jude sounding an alarm about 'certain individuals' who have 'secretly slipped in among you', who 'pervert the grace of our God into a licence for immorality and deny Jesus Christ our only Sovereign and Lord' (v. 4). The results of such compromise could not be more grim. Jude describes such individuals as 'wild waves of the sea, foaming up their shame; wandering stars, for whom blackest darkness has been reserved for ever' (v. 13).

Likewise Jesus gives a stern warning to the church in Thyatira that they 'tolerate that woman Jezebel' who 'misleads my servants into sexual immorality and the eating of food sacrificed to idols' (Rev. 2.20). The end results are graphically spelt out:

> I will cast her on a bed of suffering, and I will make those who commit adultery with her suffer intensely, unless they repent of her ways. I will strike her children dead. Then all the churches will know that I am he who searches hearts and minds, and I will repay each of you according to your deeds.
>
> (2.22-23)

The admonition could not be clearer. 'Jezebel' represents everything in the church that Babylon, as the 'Mother of All Prostitutes and Obscenities' represents in the earth (Rev. 17.5 NLT).

When we follow the ways of this world, we reap this world's judgement. It is perhaps significant that Jesus issues the same warning to the Jewish town of Capernaum that God had given to Babylon in Isaiah:

> You said in your heart,
>   'I will ascend to the heavens' ...
> But you are brought down to the realm of the dead,
>   to the depths of the pit. (Is. 14.13,15)

'And you, Capernaum, will you be lifted to the heavens? No, you will go down to Hades'. (Matt. 11.23)

Likewise the warning he gives to the church in Laodicea has strong echoes of the warning given to Babylon later in Isaiah. Babylon is a 'lover of pleasure' and 'lounging in security' (Is. 47.8); Laodicea says, 'I am rich; I have acquired wealth and do not need a thing' (Rev. 3.17). Babylon's nakedness 'will be exposed' (Is. 47.3); Laodicea's is 'shameful' and urgently needs covering (Rev. 3.18). Babylon is warned that 'a catastrophe you cannot foresee will suddenly come upon you' (Is. 47.11); Laodicea is told that 'because you are lukewarm – neither hot nor cold – I am about to spit you out of my mouth' (Rev. 3.16).

The last point is something we should notice carefully. Jesus does not apparently object to the church being either 'hot' or 'cold'. It is the *lukewarmness* that makes him angry. In this respect, today's affluent church in the West resembles the one in Laodicea more than any other in history. For Jesus to be on the *outside* of the church, having to ask to be let in (as at Laodicea) is a catastrophe of the first degree. For this reason we need to heed these warnings very carefully. If the church accommodates to Babylon, she will share in the judgement meted out upon Babylon herself.

3. Constructive Engagement

Fortunately, there is another way. Instead of lying low or caving in, we can engage with the world around us. Doing so may take a degree of flexibility and imagination on our part. Although we may seem to be caught between two parallel universes, with inverse principles and inverse laws, we are called as Christians to live consistently across both spheres with integrity, faithfulness and servanthood, turning Babel values into Bible values, and modelling Christ's example in whatever situation we find ourselves.

Our supreme model in this process is always going to be Jesus himself, whose inexhaustible reservoir of grace to others, coupled with a complete selflessness within his own spirit, offer a complete redefinition of what it means to be human, and a beacon of hope to a broken society.

His life demonstrates the true order of God's kingdom, a kingdom not of this world (John 18.36). For example, he illustrates the staggering claim at the Last Supper that 'anyone who has seen me has seen the Father' (John 14.9) by washing the feet of his disciples, a task considered too demeaning even for a Jewish servant to perform.[1] In doing so he turns every traditional notion of 'Lordship' on its head, displaying the face of an upside-down God who turns his back on the mighty but stands on the side of the weak and powerless.

The true church, then, is called to radical humility and servanthood. Unlike the top-heavy construction of Nebuchadnezzar's statue, the church is built from the *base upwards*, with Christ and the apostles at the bottom (Eph. 2.19-22). In contrast to everything represented by Babylon, we are to model an inverted kingdom where strong is weak and weak is strong. We are to prefer others before ourselves, and to place the lowliest among us on the highest pedestal. As Jesus reminds us, 'whatever you did for one of the *least* of these brothers and sisters of mine, you did for me' (Matt. 25.40).

In this sense there is something radically subversive about the gospel. In Acts 17.6 Christians are those who turn the world 'upside-down' (as translated in many versions), and this is still our mission today. From God's perspective, of course, we are actually turning the world the right way up!

So, for example, while in the world's eyes, size matters, it is not so with God. From the Old Testament, we know the story of Gideon, who had *too many* men in his army and needed to cut them down (Judges 7.2-8), and the story of David, who rejected heavy armour to rely on the simplicity of a few stones in his battle with Goliath (1 Sam. 17.38-40). Israel is promised that if she walks in obedience, 'five of you will chase a hundred, and a hundred of you will chase ten thousand' (Lev. 26.8).

Likewise, in the New Testament we hear of how five loaves and two fish were able to provide a feast for thousands of people (Matt. 14.13-21) and how the widow's tiny offering in the temple far eclipsed the lavish donations of the rich (Mark 12.41-44). We might remember that the extraordinary revival in the Hebrides in 1949, where people were literally falling to their knees in the streets, was triggered in part by two old ladies praying. God's strength is made perfect in our weakness (2 Cor. 12.9).

Similarly, while in the world's eyes, intellectual prowess matters, it is not so with God. For,

> God chose the foolish things of the world to shame the wise; God chose the weak things of the world to shame the strong. God chose the lowly things of this world and the despised things—and the things that are not—to nullify the things that are, so that no one may boast before him. It is because of him that you are in Christ Jesus, who has become for us wisdom from God—that is, our righteousness, holiness and redemption. Therefore, as it is written: "Let the one who boasts boast in the Lord." (1 Cor. 1.27-31)

Faithfulness in things of God does not depend on our position or standing within society. We can still shine out from the very bottom of the pile. Martin Luther King once said this:

If it falls your lot to be a street sweeper, sweep streets like Raphael painted pictures; sweep streets like Michelangelo carved marble; sweep streets like Beethoven composed music; sweep streets like Shakespeare wrote poetry. Sweep streets so well that all the host of heaven and earth will have to pause and say: Here lived a great street sweeper who swept his job well.[2]

In living up to our calling, God is challenging us, as much as possible, to learn to *penetrate* the prevailing culture and to engage with it wholeheartedly. Jesus ministered largely in Galilee, an area that was heavily impregnated by Greek culture rather than being purely Jewish in its makeup. Peter would have preached in Greek to Cornelius and his friends in Acts 10 to have made himself understood. John, while remaining faithful to his Jewish background, opens up common ground with the Greek idea of the 'Logos' in his gospel, and Luke likewise gears his own writings to a Gentile audience.

The same is true of Paul's ministry, as revealed in Acts. During his time in Ephesus he reasoned in the lecture-hall of Tyrannus for two years, embedding himself in the local culture (19.9-10). While in Athens, despite his distress at the level of idolatry, he did not repudiate every local belief but made efforts to find common ground (17.22-23). Elsewhere he also used his Roman citizenship to good effect (16.37-39; 22.25-29) and was successful in using the Roman system to outwit the schemes of the religious authorities in Jerusalem (25.9-11).

Paul's example shows how, in defending a Biblical worldview, we need great wisdom in the way we engage with the world. We are called to be persuasive, not confrontational:

Be wise in the way you act toward outsiders; make the most of every opportunity. Let your conversation be always full of grace, seasoned with salt, so that you may know how to answer everyone. (Col. 4.5-6)

Likewise Peter writes as follows:

> Always be prepared to give an answer to everyone who asks you to give the reason for the hope that you have. But do this with gentleness and respect, keeping a clear conscience, so that those who speak maliciously against your good behaviour in Christ may be ashamed of their slander. (1 Pet. 3.15-16).

In this respect it is very important to speak both with humility and clarity. We need to be able to articulate the reasons for our faith in straightforward, understandable ways (2 Tim. 2.25-26). In living out the gospel we are holding an olive branch out to other human beings made precious and beautiful in God's image.

We also need a profound understanding of our audience and communicate in terms which are appropriate to the context. The way Jesus talks to the Samaritan woman or the woman caught in adultery is very different to the way he talks to the Pharisees. Similarly, the way Paul engages with the Athenians or the secular leaders that he witnesses to is very different from the way he spoke to the Galatians or Corinthians in internal letters. As Paul declares:

> When I was with the Jews, I lived like a Jew to bring the Jews to Christ. … When I am with those who are weak, I share their weakness, for I want to bring the weak to Christ. Yes, I try to find common ground with everyone, doing everything I can to save some. (1 Cor. 9.20, 22 NLT)

Clearly there is a delicate balancing act to be performed. As we noted in Chapter Ten, the church needs to sound out a clear signal (like the trumpet in 1 Corinthians 14.8), and not offer a wavering, half-hearted message. And yet we need to pray for ways of articulating our message in terms that are accessible and relevant to others, even though we know that the truth we proclaim is an absolute one. Jesus showed how it is possible to be firm but compassionate, full of grace *and* truth.

We are not called, however, just to demonstrate our message in words. God wants us to *live out* his kingdom and his values so that they percolate through the secular system. The Jewish exiles are told to serve Babylon and to seek its welfare (Jer. 27.17) or face his judgement. If Babylon prospers, we in turn will prosper (29.7). In our everyday lives we are called to act without giving offence (Matt. 17.27) and to do what is right in the eyes of everyone (2 Cor. 8.21). We are to be 'children of God without fault in a warped and crooked generation' who shine out 'like stars in the sky' (Phil. 2.15). We are to live out our everyday lives in submission to the secular governing authorities (Rom. 13.1-5).

Likewise, in our positions of responsibility, we are called to serve with integrity, diligence and a humble heart. Joseph, Daniel, Nehemiah, Mordecai and Josephus reached the highest places of influence in pagan society, not through fighting their way to the top, but through waiting patiently for God's appointed time. They show us how we can display distinctiveness, not by *separating* from the world, but by *illuminating* it. Even though they worked under demonic, ungodly systems, they were not defiled any more than Jesus was defiled through eating with tax collectors and sinners.

In all that we do, we should attempt to pursue excellence in every field, as befitting anyone chosen to represent the Creator of the universe. Proverbs 22.29 declares that

> Do you see a man skilful in his work? He will stand before kings; he will not stand before obscure men.

Daniel in particular provides a perfect template for how we should interact with the culture around us. He was willing to take a pagan name and to be counted amongst the astrologers and diviners. Like his friends Shadrach, Meshach and Abednego, he was found to be ten times wiser than all the magicians in Babylon (Dan. 1.20), and it was his prompt intervention that saved the lives of all the wise men in the city (2.1-24). Moreover, he managed at the same time not to compromise on core beliefs, being bold in the things of God.

Like Joseph, he had an integrity that drew those in authority to him and invited favour. Daniel's boss, Nebuchadnezzar, had a quixotic, perhaps even a psychopathic personality (Dan. 2.12) and yet Daniel responds to the situation with tact and discretion (2.14). He behaves as a model employee and yet always gives the glory to God (2.45).[3]

The same is true at an earlier stage in Israel's history in the relationship between David and Saul. Like Nebuchadnezzar, Saul's personality can also be described as impulsive and unbalanced: he understood just as well as David that God had rejected his rule and chosen David in his place. But David recognised that submission to someone in authority does not depend on whether that person deserves their position, but rather on the *office* and *anointing* that they have been given (1 Sam 24.6). Though he knew the divine calling on his own life, he never attempted to 'help God out' by accelerating the process, but trusted God to raise him to the right position at the right time.

Saul's son Jonathan provides another outstanding example of honour, humility and deference, laying down his natural ambitions as heir to the throne in order to selflessly promote his friend and rival. He too recognised that it is God's choice which is ultimately supreme.

John the Baptist reacted similarly in the graciousness with which he steps aside for Jesus:

The friend who attends the bridegroom waits and listens for him, and is full of joy when he hears the bridegroom's voice. That joy is mine, and it is now complete. He must become greater; I must become less." (John 3.29-30).

In turn this reflects the ultimate example of Christ himself, turning aside from his own glory to secure our salvation, as we were reminded in Chapter One:

Christ Jesus …, being in very nature God,
    did not consider equality with God something to be used to
his own advantage;
rather, he made himself nothing
    by taking the very nature of a servant,
    being made in human likeness.
And being found in appearance as a man,
    he humbled himself
    by becoming obedient to death –
        even death on a cross! (Phil. 2.5-8)

Living on what might seem like a knife-edge between the world and the kingdom of God can be challenging. But in all these things, Jesus provides our perfect example of how we can fulfil both sides of the equation perfectly. When challenged by the Pharisees on whether it was lawful or not to pay taxes to Caesar, he asks them to bring him a coin and then offers a consummate reply:

'Whose image is this? And whose inscription?'
'Caesar's,' they replied.
Then he said to them, 'So give back to Caesar what is Caesar's, and to God what is God's.' (Matt. 22.20-21)

There is, of course, an irony in Jesus' answer. Within a few centuries of Jesus making this remark, it was *his* picture back of many of the imperial coins! Today, if we are to impact the world around us, he also needs to become the picture on the coin of our lives, visible to all, and whose value far exceeds any earthly currency.

This is a calling not just for each of us as individuals, but the whole people of God. At its best the church should be a demonstration to the world of the true unity of spirit that Babel so spectacularly failed to achieve (Eph. 4.3-6). She is God's direct answer to every man-made utopia and artificial attempt at oneness. We are 'the fullness of him who fills everything in every way' (Eph. 1.23). Jesus prayed that we should be one just as he and the Father are one (John 17.20-23).

True unity, then, comes through Christ himself and through no other source. The cross was the only possible means through which the brokenness of the universe could be restored:

> With all wisdom and understanding, he made known to us the mystery of his will according to his good pleasure, which he purposed in Christ, to be put into effect when the times reach their fulfilment – **to bring unity to all things** in heaven and on earth under Christ. (Eph. 1.8-10)

> For God was pleased to have all his fullness dwell in him, and through him to **reconcile to himself all things**, whether things on earth or things in heaven, by making peace through his blood, shed on the cross. (Col. 1.19-20).

We are called, therefore, to be agents of this reconciliation to the world around us (2 Cor. 5.18-20), bringing light and blessing to the secular situation in which we find ourselves.

At its heart mankind has never lost its God-given longing for the New Jerusalem. Every September at the Royal Albert Hall passionate voices are raised singing the visionary words of William Blake:

> I will not cease from mental fight,
> Nor shall my sword sleep in my hand:
> Till we have built Jerusalem,
> In England's green and pleasant Land.

Unfortunately, though the idea is an attractive one, it is completely false. The mistake, however well-intentioned, is somehow that *we* can build Jerusalem through own unaided efforts. Nothing could be further from the truth.

However, in the model prayer that he taught us, Jesus did tell us to pray for God's kingdom to come *here on earth* just as it is in heaven. It is not just a future hope, but something we are to wholeheartedly seek for *now*. To that extent, God does give each one of us a part to play in bringing about Jerusalem in the lives of those around us: in our homes, in our workplaces and in our communities. We are to be agents of transformation, even if that can never be fully complete until Jesus returns.

Ultimately we know that this age is just a shadow of what lies ahead. We are looking forward to something far greater in the future, when all of man's highest and noblest aspirations will be completely eclipsed.

The writer to the Hebrews expresses this beautifully:

> By faith Abraham, when called to go to a place he would later receive as his inheritance, obeyed and went, even though he did not know where he was going. By faith he made his home in the promised land like a stranger in a foreign country; he lived in tents, as did Isaac and Jacob, who were heirs with him of the same promise. For he was looking forward to the city with foundations, whose architect and builder is God. ...

> All these people were still living by faith when they died. They did not receive the things promised; they only saw them and welcomed them from a distance, admitting that they were foreigners and strangers on earth. People who say such things show that they are looking for a country of their own. If they had been thinking of the country they had left, they would have had opportunity to return. Instead, they were longing for a better country – a heavenly one. Therefore God is not ashamed to be called their God, for he has prepared a city for them.
>
> (Heb. 11.8-10, 13-16)

Since the opening of this book we have explored the conflict between Babel and Bible through its many twists and turns, and the battle for the soul of mankind. In our struggles today we stand on the shoulders of many saints in the Old and New Testaments who have gone before us.

From our viewpoint today, however, we have the extraordinary advantage of knowing how the Bible ends. The 'great symphony' that we described in Chapter Three reaches its triumphant climax. Babylon finally falls and the kingdom of God enters its full consummation. The curse of Eden is reversed and Paradise is restored.

God has a wonderful way of righting wrongs and putting things right in his own perfect timing. At the moment we still live in an age of transition, attempting to live out the kingdom while awaiting its complete fulfilment. But we have one certain hope which is emphatically spelt in the New Testament: the King is coming, and creation will be transformed by his reign:

> Then I saw 'a new heaven and a new earth,' for the first heaven and the first earth had passed away, and there was no longer any sea. I saw the Holy City, the new Jerusalem, coming down out of heaven from God, prepared as a bride beautifully dressed for her husband. And I heard a loud voice from the throne saying, 'Look! God's dwelling-place is now among the people, and he will dwell with them. They will be his people, and God himself will be with them and be their God. "He will wipe every tear from their eyes. There will be no more death or mourning or crying or pain, for the old order of things has passed away.' (Rev. 21.1-4)

Let us not get discouraged as we wait for this moment to dawn. Rather, let us keep our eyes fixed on Jesus, and persevere as we continue our daily pilgrimage towards the New Jerusalem, where all the longings of our hearts will be fulfilled. We can so easily lose heart when we focus on our present trials. But the Bible encourages to look up into the far distance, to join with the great cloud of witnesses that have gone before us into heaven, and rank after rank of angels, and cry out with one accord, 'Amen. Come, Lord Jesus.'

Questions to Consider:

(i)   In 2 Timothy 4.9-18 Paul feels abandoned by many of his companions. Some of them have run away and others have caved in to the comforts of the world. How can we train ourselves to remain firm under heavy pressure?

(ii)   Read Esther 3.8-5.8 and 7.1-10. How can we learn from Esther's courage in risking everything to turn a calamitous situation around? To what degree has each one us been put in place for 'such a time as this' (4.14)?

(iii)   We have read how John the Baptist said of Jesus, 'He must become greater; I must become less (John 3.30).' How can we let this work through our lives on a daily basis? Are we yet able to say, with Paul, that 'I have been crucified with Christ and I no longer live, but Christ lives in me' (Gal 2.20)?

ENDNOTES TO EACH CHAPTER

Introduction

[1] I appreciate that many (often legitimate) criticisms have been levelled at this revised translation, but it remains the version in widest contemporary use outside the King James Version.

Chapter Two: A Tale of Two Trees

[1] Derek Kidner, *Genesis: an Introduction and Commmentary* (London: Tyndale Press, 1967), p.36.

Chapter Three: A Tale of Two Women

[1] William Harris Rule, *Oriental Records Monumental: Confirmatory of the Old Testament Scriptures* (London: Bagster and Sons, 1877), p. 35-36.
[2] https://www.britishmuseum.org/collection/object/W_1938-0520-1
[3] Edward Granville Browne, *Revised Translation of Chahár Maqála ("Four discourses") of Nizámi-i-'Arúdi af-Samarqand* (Cambridge: CUP 1921), p. 91-93.

[4] R.K. Harrison, *Introduction to the Old Testament* (London: Tyndale Press, 1969), p. 1116-1117.

[5] See Gerhard F. Hasel 'The Book of Daniel: Evidences Relating to Persons and Chronology', in Andrews University Seminary Studies, Vol. 19, No. 1 (Spring 1981), p.41-42 at https://www.andrews.edu/library/car/cardigital/Periodicals /AUSS/1981-1/1981-1-03.pdf.

Chapter Four: The Emperor's New Clothes

[1] There is a possibility that 'uncovering his father's nakedness' has a sexual connotation here, as it does in Leviticus 18.6, 20.11, and 20.17. This possibility is discussed in the Talmud (b.Sanhedrin 70a). Certainly incest is the direct result of drunkenness in Genesis 19.30-35.

Chapter Five: From Abel to Babel

[1] Alec Motyer, *Look to the Rock*, (London: IVP 1996), p.128.

[2] Book of Jubilees, 10.21.

[3] Louis Ginzberg, *Legends of the Jews*, Vol. 1: Bible Times and Characters from the Creation to Jacob (Philadelphia: Jewish Publication Society of America, 1909), p.179.

[4] In the Talmud this appears at b.Sanhedrin 109a; the same idea is also found in the Targum Pseudo-Jonathan and the Targum Neofiti to Genesis 11.4, and in 3 Baruch 2.7.

[5] James Frazer, *Folklore in the Old Testament: Studies in Comparative Religion, Legend and Law* (London: Macmillan, 1918), p. 381-2.

[6] James Frazer, *op. cit.*, p. 383-4.

[7] See Petros Koutoupis, 'Gateway to the Heavens: The Assyrian Account to the Tower of Babel', posted on June 13, 2014 at https://www.ancient-origins.net/myths-legends-asia/gateway-heavens-assyrian-account-tower-babel-001751.

[8] Herodotus, *Histories*, 1.178.

[9] William Harris Rule, *op. cit.*, p. 35-36.

[10] Herodotus, *op. cit.* 1.181.

Chapter Six: The Dream that Unlocks History

[1] Many modern scholars prefer the designations Babylon, Media, Persia and Greece. However, since Media never existed as a separate empire after the fall of Babylon, this interpretation seems difficult to defend. Furthermore, the description of Greece seems to fit better with the four wings of the third creature in the corresponding vision in Daniel 7.6, as the Greek Empire was split into four parts after the death of Alexander the Great.

[2] Sybilline Oracles 4.49-110 and 231-248; Book of Enoch, 93.2-10 and 91.12-17.

[3] Hesiod, *Works and Days*, 109 -201.

[4] Ovid, *Metamorphoses*, 1.89 -150.

[5] Sefer Hayashar, 8.17-19.

[6] Genesis Rabbah, 38.11.

[7] Tacitus, *Histories*, 5.20.

[8] Josephus, *Jewish War*, 2.14.

[9] See *Father, Forgive Us: A Christian Response to the Church's Heritage of Jewish Persecution* by Fred Wright (Monarch, 2002).

[10] David Lambourn, *The Forgotten Bride: How the Church Betrayed its Jewish Heritage* (London: KDP, 2019), p.56.

Chapter Seven: A Kingdom Divided

[1] Frank McLynn, *Napoleon: A Biography*, (New York: Arcade Publishing, 2002), p. 664.

[2] Sir Robert Anderson, *The Coming Prince*, 10th Edition (Grand Rapids, MI: Kregel, 1957), p.276-77; David Pawson, *Unlocking the Bible*, Omnibus Edition (London: HarperCollins, 2003), p. 658.

Chapter Eight: The Shock of the New

[1] James Keller, *Chamber Music: A Listener's Guide*, (Oxford: OUP 2010), p.488.

[2] Albert Kirk Grayson, *Babylonian Historical-Literary Texts* (Toronto: University of Toronto Press, 1975), p.4.

[3] Interview with Maureen Cleave in the *London Evening Standard*, March 4 1966.
[4] https://www.popularmechanics.com/technology/a8562/ins ide-the-future-how-popmech-predicted-the-next-110-years-14831802/.
[5] Daniel Druckman; Jerome E Singer; Harold Van Cott, *Enhancing Organizational Performance* (Washington, D.C.: National Academies Press, 1997), p.2.
[6] See https://www.kurzweilai.net/the-law-of-accelerating-returns.
[7] See Elon Musk, 'An integrated brain-machine interface platform with thousands of channels' at https://www.biorxiv.org/content/10.1101/703801v1.full, posted July 17 2019.
[8] See https://neuralink.com/applications/.
[9] Karl Marx, 'A Contribution to the Critique of Hegel's Philosophy of Right', written in December 1843-January 1844, and first published in Deutsch-Französische Jahrbücher, (Paris: February 7 and 10 1844).

Chapter Nine: The Axe that Raised Itself

[1] David Pawson, *op. cit.*, p.459.
[2] Josephus, *Against Apion*, 1.2.
[3] René Descartes, *Discours de la Methode* (Leyden: Jan Maire, 1637), p.32.
[4] Thomas Paine, *The Age of Reason*, (New York: G.N. Devries, 1827), p.6.
[5] Friedrich Nietzsche, *The Gay Science*, Vol. 3, section 125, in Cambridge Texts in the History of Philosophy, trans. Josefine Nauckhoff (CUP: Cambridge, 2001), p.120.
[6] Quoted from Charles T. Cullen, *Jefferson's Extracts from the Gospels: The Papers of Thomas Jefferson*, Second Series (Princeton, NJ: Princeton University Press, 1983), p.409.
[7] Thomas Huxley, writing in the Fortnightly Review (London: February 1869), p.141.

[8] Brian Wheeler, 'What Happens at an Atheist Church?' posted at www.bbc.co.uk › news › magazine-21319945
[9] Letter to Maxim Gorki dated November 13/14 1913, quoted by Robert Conquest in *The Harvest of Sorrow: Soviet Collectivisation and the Terror-Famine* (London: Hutchinson, 1986), p.199.
[10] Mikhail Bakunin (1871) 'God and the State' in *The Communist Manifesto and Other Revolutionary Writings: Marx, Marat, Paine, Mao, Gandhi, and others*, ed. Bob Blaisdell, (Mineola, NY: Dover, 2012), p.191.
[11] https://www.pewforum.org/2015/05/12/chapter-3-demographic-profiles-of-religious-groups/
[12] Christopher Hitchens, *The Portable Atheist: Essential Readings for the Nonbeliever* (London: Da Capo Press, 2007), p. 6. It also might be enlightening in this instance to look at Scott A. McGreal, 'Why Religious People Are Less Likely to Own Cats', which was posted on June 7 2020 in *Psychology Today* (https://www.psychologytoday.com/us/blog/unique-everybody-else/202006/why-religious-people-are-less-likely-own-cats).

Chapter Ten: The Gender Agenda

[1] Alec Motyer, *op. cit.*, p.70.
[2] John Stott, *Issues facing Christians today,* Revised Edition (London: Marshall Pickering, 1990), p.346 (a similar idea appears in Plato's *Symposium*).
[3] Joseph Haydn and Benjamin Vincent**,** *Haydn's Dictionary of Dates: and Universal Information relating to all Ages and Nations, containing the History of the World to August, 1873*, 14th Edition (London: Moxon 1873), p.211.
[4] https://www.ons.gov.uk/peoplepopulationandcommunity/birthsdeathsandmarriages/divorce/bulletins/divorcesinenglandandwales/2018#.
[5] The Hebrew word that is used in in Daniel 11.31 and 12.11 for 'the abomination that causes desolation' is not identical to the one used in Leviticus 18.22 and 20.13, but shares the same

underlying root, while the word used in the Greek translation of Daniel's phrase in Matthew 24.15 and Mark 13.14 is the same one used in Revelation 17.14-15.

[6] Shulamith Firestone, 'The Dialectic of Sex' in *Radical Feminism: A Documentary Reader*, ed. Barbara A. Crow (New York: New York University Press, 1999), p.95.

[7] While the Democratic Unionist Party were propping up the British government under the premiership of Theresa May between 2017 and 2019, it was their views on Biblical creation which were most often linked to their views on gay marriage as being particularly offensive to educated opinion.

[8] In particular, Seth's son is said to be in the image of Adam (Gen. 5.3) just as Adam is in the image of God (1.26-27).

[9] Tom Williams, 'Midwives told to say chestfeeding instead of breast feeding to be more inclusive', *Metro*, February 10 2021.

Chapter Eleven: The Miracle of Common Grace

[1] Augustine of Hippo, 'The City of God', 18.22.

[2] Gandhi once declared that 'he was certainly the highest example of one who wished to give everything, asking nothing in return, and not caring what creed might happen to be professed by the recipient … To me, he was one of the greatest teachers humanity has ever had.' ('What Jesus Means to Me' in The Modern Review, October 1941, p.406).

[3] Philo, *On the Confusion of Tongues*, 108.

[4] David Lambourn, *But is He God?* (Paternoster: Milton Keynes 2014), p.72.

[5] Philo, *That God is Unchangeable*, 176.

[6] Winston Churchill, 'The Gift of a Common Tongue', speech given at Harvard University on September 6 1943, transcribed at https://winstonchurchill.org/resources/speeches/1941-1945-war-leader/the-price-of-greatness-is-responsibility/.

[7] As David Pawson points out (*op. cit.*, p.499), such an outcome is unlikely to be achieved with the omission of the first part of the verse, which refers to God acting in sovereign power among the nations as judge.

Chapter Twelve: The Lights of the Metropolis

[1] See Jessa Gamble, 'How do you build a city in space?' in *The Guardian*, May 16 2014, and https://www.inverse.com/innovation/mars-city-spacex-story
[2] b.Sanhedrin 109a; a similar image appears in 3 Baruch 3.7-8.
[3] Martial, *Epigrams,* 7.20.
[4] Doris Behrens-Abouseif , *Islamic Architecture in Cairo: An Introduction* (Leiden: Brill, 1992), p.6.
[5] Claudia Geib, 'The UAE Released a VR Tour of the First City on Mars', posted November 29 2017 at https://futurism.com/uae-released-vr-tour-first-city-mars
[6] Rabbi Allen S. Maller, 'The Qur'an and Torah on the True Meaning of the Tower of Babel and Multiple Languages', posted September 29 2018 at https://www.ancient-origins.net/myths-legends-europe/meaning-tower-babel-0010770.

Chapter Fourteen: Babylon in the Church

[1] Vance Havner, in his Facebook post on 31st July 2012.
[2] This assumes the so-called 'South Galatian' view of the letter which would date it around 49 AD, around the time of the Council of Jerusalem. An alternative 'North Galatian' view would place it roughly contemporary with Romans, around 57 AD, and therefore after the dissension with Barnabas.
[3] For example, Justin Martyr appears to sanction the worship of angels in his *First Apology* 6, and Origen in *Contra Celsum* 8.13.
[4] Rudolf Bultmann 'New Testament and Mythology' in *Kerygma and Myth*, ed. Hans Bartsch (New York: Harper 1961) p. 2-3.
[5] http://abcnews.go.com/m/story?id=89965.
[6] 'Jeremy Paxman on the Church of England's fight to survive' in *FT Magazine*, September 6 2017.
[7] 'Conservative Evangelicals claim there are serious errors in the Church of England', The Christian News, April 15 1985.

[8] From John Boyle O'Reilly, 'In Bohemia', in James Jeffrey Roche, *Life Of John Boyle O'Reilly, together with his Complete Poems and Speeches*, (New York: Cassell, 1891), p.445.

[9] Justo L González and Catherine Gunsalus González, *The Liberating Pulpit* (Nashville: Abingdon Press, 1994), p.16-17.

[10] Eusebius, *Life of Constantine*, 3.18.

[11] It is easy to see why. She is set on 'seven hills' (v. 9) a clear reference to Rome, and sits 'on many waters' (17.1 ESV), explained as 'peoples, multitudes, nations and languages' (v. 15). She is described as being 'dressed in purple and scarlet', and 'glittering with gold, precious stones and pearls', while holding a 'golden cup in her hand, filled with abominable things' (v. 4). Most of all, she is said to be 'drunk with the blood of God's holy people, the blood of those who bore testimony to Jesus' (v. 6).

[12] 'Denmark - Bureau of Democracy, Human Rights, and Labor' in International Religious Freedom Report 2009 (U.S. Department of State, 2009), and, for more information, https://www.km.dk/folkekirken/kirkestatistik/folkekirkens-medlemstal/.

[13] It is striking that the two men who almost single-handedly transformed the life of this 1740), p. 2. country during the 18th century, John Wesley and George Whitefield, had to do so outside the Anglican fold. Whitefield accused a former Archbishop of Canterbury, John Tillotson, of knowing 'no more of Christianity than Mahomet' in *Three Letters from the Reverend Mr. G. Whitefield*, (Philadelphia: printed and sold by B. Franklin, **Chapter Fifteen: Babylon Transformed?**

[1] Mekilta on Exodus 21.2.

[2] Speech on December 5 1957, quoted by Wolfgang Mieder in *"Making a Way Out of No Way": Martin Luther King's Sermonic Proverbial Rhetoric* (New York: Peter Lang, 2010), p. 449.

[3] Daniel's life and example provided a perfect model for many Nestorian Christians who helped to contribute to the so-called 'Golden Age' of Islamic civilization in Baghdad during the

reign of the Ummayads and the Abbasids by translating works of leading textbooks of science , medicine and philosophy from Greek into Arabic. Between the 8th and 11th centuries, eight generations of the Nestorian Bukhtishu dynasty served as private physicians to caliphs and sultans.

OTHER PUBLICATIONS BY THIS AUTHOR:

But is he God? (Authentic Media, 2014)

The idea that the creator of the universe should come to earth as a human being and die on a wooden cross is one of the most extraordinary claims made by any world religion. But is it true? This comprehensive survey sifts through all the evidence to find the answer to one of the most important questions that has ever been asked.

'A very readable and exciting examination of the greatest figure in human history.'
Lord Carey, 103rd Archbishop of Canterbury

The Forgotten Bride (Amazon KDP, 2019)

Are God's purposes for the Jewish people finished? Is the church the 'new Israel'? Many believers would answer 'yes' to both questions, but what does the Bible say? This book considers the consequences of 'replacement theology', covering both the horrific treatment of the Jews by the church for two thousand years and the response we need to make today. It challenges the church to repent, to re-engage with the complete message of the Bible, and to explore afresh its long-lost Jewish roots, in order to recover its own spiritual DNA and to counter the robust challenges it faces on many fronts today.

Fingerprint (Amazon KDP, 2022)

The fingerprints of God's design are apparent throughout the Bible and across the universe, with extraordinary correlations at every level. The book takes readers on a journey through the fascinating world of patterns and numbers in scripture and how they can impact the way that we live. This beautifully illustrated, full-colour book would make an ideal gift for baptism or confirmation and will be a treasured possession for anyone for years to come.

Printed in Great Britain
by Amazon